THE AMERICAN KENNEL CLUB'S
Meet the
Golden™

The Responsible Dog Owner's Handbook

AKC's Meet the Breeds Series

BOWTIE
P R E S S®

Irvine, California
A Division of BowTie, Inc.

AN OFFICIAL PUBLICATION OF **AKC** THE AMERICAN KENNEL CLUB

AMERICAN
KENNEL CLUB

Brought to you by The American Kennel Club and The Golden Retriever Club of America.
Lead Editor: Karen Julian
Art Director: Cindy Kassebaum
Production Manager: Laurie Panaggio
Production Supervisor: Jessica Jaensch
Production Coordinator: Leah Rosalez

Vice President, Chief Content Officer: June Kikuchi
Vice President, Kennel Club Books: Andrew DePrisco
BowTie Press: Jennifer Calvert, Amy Deputato, Karen Julian, Jarelle S. Stein

Photographs by: Gina Cioli/BowTie Studio: 10, 14, 28, 31, 33, 40, 42, 67, 72, 84, 86, 94, 109, 120; Cheryl Ertelt: Cover inset, 3, 4, 12, 24, 29, 30, 41, 77, 87, 106, 115; Christopher Appoldt Photography: Cover, Back cover, 4, 13, 46, 47, 50-51, 54, 56, 64, 68, 69; Cris Kelly Photography: Cover inset, 43, 60, 112-113, 121; Fox Hill Photo: Daniel Johnson, 35, 96; Paulette Johnson, 52, 58, 66, 89, 95, 97; Connie Summers/Paulette Johnson, 78; Gondolin Photography (Christopher Butler): 20-21; LMEimages (Laurie Meehan-Elmer): 6-7, 34, 36, 45, 82-83, 108, 110; Mark Raycroft Photography: Cover insets, 4, 8, 9, 15, 16-17, 18, 22, 25, 26-27, 37, 38-39, 44, 48, 49, 53, 57, 59, 61, 62-63, 92-93, 105, 114, 119; PawPrince Studios (Pamela Marks): 23, 32, 73, 79, 88, 98; Shutterstock: 55, 65, 75, 81, 85, 99, 118, 124; Sporthorse Photography (Tara Gregg): 1, 11, 70-71, 74, 76, 80, 90, 101, 102-103, 111, 116.

BowTie Press®
Division of BOWTIE INC.
3 Burroughs, Irvine, CA 92618

Library of Congress Cataloging-in-Publication Data

The American Kennel Club's meet the golden : the responsible dog owner's handbook.
    p. cm. -- (AKC's meet the breeds series)
 Includes bibliographical references and index.
 ISBN 978-1-935484-88-2
 1. Golden retriever. I. American Kennel Club.
 SF429.G63A44 2012
 636.752'7--dc23

                        2012007688

Printed and bound in the United States
16 15 14 13 12   2 3 4 5 6 7 8 9 10

Meet Your New Dog

Welcome to *Meet the Golden*. Whether you're a long-time Golden Retriever owner, or you've just brought home your first puppy, we wish you a lifetime of happiness and enjoyment with your new pet.

In this book, you'll learn about the history of the breed, receive tips on feeding, grooming, and training, and learn about all the fun you can have with your dog. The American Kennel Club and BowTie Press hope that this book serves as a useful guide on the lifelong journey you'll take with your canine companion.

Owned and cherished by millions across America, Golden Retrievers make wonderful companions that also enjoy taking part in a variety of dog sports, including Conformation (dog shows), Obedience, Rally®, and Agility.

Thousands of Goldens have also earned the AKC Canine Good Citizen® award by demonstrating their good manners at home and in the community. We hope that you and your Golden will become involved in AKC events, too! Learn how to get involved at www.akc .org/events or find a training club in your area at www.akc.org/events/trainingclubs.cfm.

We encourage you to connect with other Golden owners on the AKC website (www.akc .org), Facebook (www.facebook.com/american kennelclub), and Twitter (@akcdoglovers). Also visit the website for the Golden Retriever Club of America (www.grca.org), the national parent club for the Golden Retriever, to learn about the breed from reputable exhibitors and breeders.

Enjoy *Meet the Golden*!

Sincerely,

Dennis B. Sprung
AKC President and CEO

6

26

50

102

Contents

CHAPTER ONE

More Precious than Gold

Is your dream dog friendly, energetic, smart, and covered in a shimmering golden coat? Then the Golden Retriever is the perfect dog for you! Bred by a British nobleman in the nineteenth century to hunt waterfowl, this breed has become one of the most recognized, beloved, and talented dogs in the world. The Golden is truly a wonder dog that guides the blind; assists the disabled; sniffs out bombs, drugs, and cancer cells; searches (and rescues!) people buried in the aftermath of natural disasters and

Always the Bridesmaid

The Golden Retriever is in the top five AKC registered breeds but has never beaten the most popular breed, the Labrador Retriever. To register your Golden pup with the AKC, fill out the Dog Registration Application you were given by your breeder and mail it to the AKC office in North Carolina. You can also register your dog online at www.akc.org.

terrorist attacks; and brings smiles to the faces of children and seniors in hospitals and nursing homes. Plus he's one swell chum to his human family.

You can see the smiling face of Goldens on television commercials, magazine advertisements, birthday greeting cards, T-shirts, kitchen magnets, wallpapers for computers—virtually everywhere imaginable. People can't seem to get enough of the Golden Retriever. Not only has the Golden been in the top five most popular breeds in the United States for over three decades, according to American Kennel Club registration statistics, but the breed ranks high in England, Japan, China, Sweden, and Norway as well.

ARE YOU RIGHT FOR AN 18-KARAT GOLDEN?

Anyone who's owned (or been owned by) a Golden will attest that this breed is the ideal family dog and companion. A better canine friend cannot be found. Golden Retrievers might be all-around, do-it-all dogs, but you must remember that every dog has his own distinct personality, and in a breed as versatile as the Golden, you can find individual dogs with extremely different personalities and abilities.

"Friendly" is actually in the definition of the breed, and Goldens make everyone they meet feel like a long-lost friend. They greet family members, postal carriers, and kind strangers with tail-wagging enthusiasm. This quality makes

Goldens have the need to retrieve and will happily play fetch for hours. Channel your Golden's energy into obedience training.

Lovable, huggable Golden Retrievers are popular not only in the United States, but in Europe and Asia as well.

the Golden Retriever a wonderful therapy dog that visits patients in care facilities, veterans' hospitals, and assisted-living communities. This quality has also led the breed to excel as guide and assistance dogs, bonding with their caretakers regardless of their physical limitations.

Few breeds surpass the Golden's zest for life. He finds joy in every moment of the day, exploring every hole and corner of the yard, and retrieving every stick and leaf he can find. Like all other retrievers, Goldens love to mouth. They will retrieve anything within their reach—socks, underwear, leather belts, and their absolute favorite, anything made of feathers (down comforters, jackets, pillows, and the occasional feather boa). Unchecked, they will shred these things to pieces. Many Golden Retriever puppies are miniature chewing machines. Some chew their way well into adulthood, leaving telltale scars on furniture and cabinetry. Conscientious owners quickly learn to keep everything off the floor and away from puppies, adults, and senior Goldens. If you're waiting for your puppy to mature and grow out of his "I-love-feathers" phase, don't hold your breath!

Wise owners minimize damage around the home with diligent supervision, providing appropriate chew toys, and teaching their Golden Retriever puppy what he may and may not chew. Owners who fail to dog-proof their homes or supervise their puppies tell horror stories of the impossible things their Goldens have consumed or destroyed.

Did You Know?

The Golden Retriever breed migrated to the United States in the early 1900s and gained official American Kennel Club (AKC) recognition in 1925. The first Golden registered with the AKC was Lomberdale Blondin in 1925.

The glory of your Golden Retriever's luxuriant coat is a mixed blessing, as it sheds twice a year and transforms into golden tumbleweeds of doggy fur. The fuzz of a Golden puppy will blossom into a thick, medium-length coat that will require frequent brushing to keep it clean and manageable. Shedding periods in the spring and fall are heavy and can last about three weeks; however, Goldens shed the other forty-six weeks of the year, too! Dedicated (dog- and house-proud) owners devote at least ten minutes every other day brushing their dogs, and twenty minutes on the days in between vacuuming floors and furniture. And don't forget those muddy paws, tromping through your garden and across your kitchen floor. Few Golden Retriever homes have spotless tiled floors. If you're really fussy about a tidy house, there are other dog breeds with less coat.

The shimmery coat of the Golden Retriever is one of the breed's most recognizable characteristics. Keeping the coat looking good requires a lot of work.

HIGH-ENERGY EXPECTATIONS

Goldens are not for lazy dog lovers. A member of the Sporting Group, the Golden is a natural athlete and requires a lot of daily exercise. They enjoy lively outdoor fun and games, which are excellent outlets for their energy and enthusiasm.

Originally developed as a hunting dog expected to work all day, a Golden left alone for hours on end in the backyard with a half-eaten Frisbee or in the kitchen with a king-size Kong will quickly get bored—but not for long! Soon he'll

Get to Know the AKC

The country's leading canine organization, the American Kennel Club is a not-for-profit organization dedicated to the betterment and promotion of purebred dogs as family companions. The AKC is the largest and most prestigious dog registry in the United States. It was founded in 1884 with the mission of "upholding its registry and promoting the sport of purebred dogs and breeding for type and function." Supporting everything from health and wellness to breeding standards to fun activities for the whole family, the AKC thrives on the participation of dog lovers like you.

Help continue the legacy by registering your purebred Golden Retriever with the AKC. It's as simple as filling out the Dog Registration Application you received when you bought your puppy and mailing it to the AKC in North Carolina, or register online at www.akc.org/reg.

Tweedmouth's Dream Dog

The Golden Retriever is a man-made breed, and the man behind it all was the first Lord Tweedmouth of Guisachan, sometimes known in history books as Sir Dudley Marjoribanks. It was Tweedmouth's dream to have a superior yellow retriever to hunt ducks in the icy waters off the coast of Scotland. In pursuit of his dream dog, he paired a yellow Wavy-Coated Retriever with a Tweed Water Spaniel, both extinct ancestors of the Flat-Coated Retriever and the Curly-Coated Retriever. Tweedmouth's breeding program focused on the golden color, a people-loving temperament, and a water-loving ability, resulting in today's much-loved Golden Retriever.

begin to make his own sort of "fun." Your dog's definition of "fun" often leads to destruction and disaster. Golden Retrievers have been known to redesign entire landscapes, dig up perennial gardens, remodel the living room furniture, and eat paneling and wallpaper.

Your dog wants nothing more than time spent outdoors with his family. He is not a loner. In fact, Goldens are pretty miserable when left alone. Keep your dog smiling by being an active part of his daily life, and give him opportunities to impress you with his real talents. The American Kennel Club has many activities that Goldens excel in, from dog shows and agility to obedience, field trials, hunting tests, and much more.

The Golden Retriever is considered a medium- to large-sized breed, with males standing 23 to 24 inches in height at the withers (shoulders) and weighing 65 to 75 pounds, and females 21½ to 22½ inches in height and weighing 55 to 65 pounds. Golden Retrievers are great with children, but they can be especially exuberant, so both dog and kids must be supervised to prevent mishaps due to normal Golden rowdiness. A 75-pound adult male—barreling happily forward—can topple a full-grown adult just as easily as he can a child or a senior. This is a lot of canine to handle, so training and discipline must be high priorities on the Golden owner's to-do list.

BORN TO HUNT

Yes, it's true that many pet Golden Retrievers only retrieve Frisbees or newspapers, and they're perfectly happy doing so. Yet, the breed today continues to be bred for its original purpose of hunting upland waterfowl, such as small ducks, grouse, and partridge to large Canada geese, pheasants, and snow geese. It takes a strong, determined dog to carry a 20-pound goose through freezing water back

Golden Retrievers were originally bred as water-loving hunting dogs that retrieved waterfowl like ducks and geese. Today, Goldens are bred as show dogs and working dogs—versatile beauties with brains to spare.

to his owner. Many breeders specialize in producing super-charged hunting dogs, which can be too much for the average pet owner to handle. These Golden Retrievers have more drive and determination than show dogs and appear a bit racier and less coated.

Show breeders concentrate on ensuring that their dogs conform to the breed standard, the written description of the ideal Golden Retriever, in addition to retriever instincts. These breeders desire such qualities as a broad head, properly angulated front assembly, and a thick coat.

All Golden breeders should produce sound, healthy puppies with the friendly temperament that defines this very special breed. Pet owners generally favor Goldens that show breeders produce because the dog is more laid-back and

Responsible Pet Ownership

AMERICAN KENNEL CLUB

Getting a dog is exciting, but it's also a huge responsibility. That's why it's important to educate yourself on all that is involved in being a good pet owner. As a part of the Canine Good Citizen® test, the AKC has a "Responsible Dog Owner's Pledge," which states:

I will be responsible for my dog's health needs.

☐ I will provide routine veterinary care, including check-ups and vaccines.

☐ I will offer adequate nutrition through proper diet and clean water at all times.

☐ I will give daily exercise and regularly bathe and groom.

I will be responsible for my dog's safety.

☐ I will properly control my dog by providing fencing where appropriate, by not letting my dog run loose, and by using a leash in public.

☐ I will ensure that my dog has some form of identification when appropriate (which may include collar tags, tattoos, or microchip identification).

☐ I will provide adequate supervision when my dog and children are together.

I will not allow my dog to infringe on the rights of others.

☐ I will not allow my dog to run loose in the neighborhood.

☐ I will not allow my dog to be a nuisance to others by barking while in the yard, in a hotel room, etc.

☐ I will pick up and properly dispose of my dog's waste in all public areas, such as on the grounds of hotels, on sidewalks, in parks, etc.

☐ I will pick up and properly dispose of my dog's waste in wilderness areas, on hiking trails, on campgrounds, and in off-leash parks.

I will be responsible for my dog's quality of life.

☐ I understand that basic training is beneficial to all dogs.

☐ I will give my dog attention and playtime.

☐ I understand that owning a dog is a commitment in time and caring.

Search and Rescue Hero

The Golden Retriever's strong desire to please its owner and its unlimited love of people is manifested in its superiority in search and rescue work. The Golden has labored valiantly during many disasters, notably the September 11th terrorist attacks; Hurricane Katrina; and earthquakes in Chile, Japan, and Haiti. The cover of the best-seller, *Dog Heroes of September 11th*, proudly bears the image of a Golden resting alongside a New York firefighter.

Whether you participate in obedience, agility, or therapy work, or if you just visit the dog park every weekend, your Golden Retriever will appreciate the time spent with you, his favorite human.

generally less intense and easier to handle and train than those bred strictly for hunting. But don't be fooled, even a well-bred puppy from a good show breeder can be a handful. His enthusiasm and zest for life can easily overwhelm a novice owner who is unprepared for the breed's natural bounce-off-the-walls vitality. Perhaps due to the Goldens' high public profile, many people are unaware that the breed requires rigorous training, no matter how naturally smart he is. Like most other Sporting dogs, the Golden is more than anxious to please his owner, but he needs to learn how to do that. Obedience training is the only route to transforming an exuberant Golden into a well-behaved companion.

Structure and sound movement are important in every Golden Retriever. Whether your dog is dashing after a fallen pheasant, gaiting confidently next to you in the show ring, or pouncing on leaves falling from the maple tree in your front yard, he needs to be able to run effortlessly to "do his job." He also needs to be friendly and biddable, traits that all breeders strive for, regardless of their emphasis on the show ring or the field.

THE WELL-ROUNDED GOLDEN

Golden Retrievers really can do anything. Lots of Goldens are dual titled, meaning they hold titles in conformation (dog shows) as well as performance, such as obedience, agility, or hunt tests. The Golden is not just a pretty face smiling from the Best in Show circle. He is a working dog that can hunt all day, participate in sports, and learn to do just about anything any other dog can do—and probably better. To learn more about this sweet, fun-loving breed, go to the American Kennel Club website at www.akc.org, or check out the Golden Retriever Club of America's website at www.grca.org.

Not sure if your lifestyle is right for a high-energy Golden Retriever? Thoroughly research the breed before deciding on getting one.

At a Glance ...

Golden Retrievers are friendly and trustworthy. This loyal breed is the ultimate family dog. With proper training, the Golden can become a cherished member of your family for a lifetime.

. . . .

The Golden Retriever is not a lazy owner's dog. As a Sporting breed, the Golden requires lots of exercise and outdoor activity. Not a runner? Hate the outdoors? Have a small apartment? The fun-loving Golden Retriever may not be the right dog for you. Research the breed and talk with other owners before deciding on a Golden Retriever.

. . . .

The Golden Retriever excels in a variety of sports and activities due to his energetic and eager-to-please personality. Goldens are one of the most popular choices for service dogs, as well as therapy and search and rescue dogs. Check out all of the opportunities to get involved with your Golden at www.akc.org or www.grca.org.

CHAPTER TWO

Golden by Design

What makes one Golden Retriever look so much like the next? If you've ever been to a dog show or watched one on television, you've seen a stellar lineup of champion Goldens. As you look down the lineup, a bevy of blonde and golden beauties, you should be struck by the "sameness" of the dogs. Every head broad and slightly arched; every ear the same shape and falling close to the cheek; every coat, a rich lustrous

Goldens of all ages share certain characteristics inherent to the breed such as a golden coat, dark eyes, and a friendly personality.

golden color, lying close to the body; and every tail feather uniformly waving with enthusiasm. This "sameness" is no mere coincidence—it's absolutely by design or, shall we say, by the standard.

THE GOLD STANDARD

The breed standard describes in great detail the qualities that make the Golden Retriever distinct in conformation, ability, and character. Breeders and judges call these qualities "type," and it is type that defines a breed and makes it recognizable. Written by the Golden Retriever Club of America, the breed standard sets forth guidelines used by judges in conformation (dog shows) and by breeders in planning their breeding programs. Using the parent club's "blueprint" as their

A PIECE OF HISTORY

A minor controversy during the 2011 Christmas holiday occurred when Monsignor Robert Ritchie included an Italian sculpture of his own Golden Retriever, Lexington, in the nativity scene at St. Patrick's Cathedral in New York City. Ritchie believed that man's best friend had a place alongside the stable animals, though he conceded that the Golden Retriever was anachronistic in BC Bethlehem.

guide, breeders are able to produce dogs that are typical, sound specimens of the breed, and judges are able to select their winners by choosing the dogs that most closely conform to the ideal dog as described in the standard. Without a breed standard, the Golden Retriever would eventually lose its "type," all those qualities that make it "golden."

ROOTS OF A RETRIEVER

The Golden was originally developed as a hunting dog with very specific abilities. The first paragraph of the standard, "General Appearance," emphasizes the importance of the "retriever" in the breed's name: "A symmetrical, powerful, active dog, sound and well put together, not clumsy nor long in the leg, displaying a kindly expression and possessing a personality that is eager, alert and self-confident. Primarily a hunting dog, he should be shown in hard working condition."

Most Goldens have given up retrieving pheasants for carrying in the morning paper from the driveway or your slippers from the bedroom. One thing's for sure, the retrieving instinct is alive and strong in Golden Retrievers, so fill your dog's toy chest with Frisbees, tennis balls, stuffed animals, and other things that you can toss and he can bring back to you.

All Golden Retrievers—hunters, hikers, backyard warriors—should look like the dog the standard describes: athletic, muscular, and in hard working physical condition. The Golden also must be well put together in order to partake in high-energy sporting activities, whether agility and field competition or dog-park tennis-ball fetching.

What You See

Size and proportion, like structure, movement, and temperament, are extremely important to the breed, with males 23 to 24 inches in height at the withers

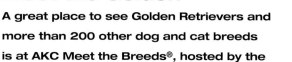

Meet the Golden

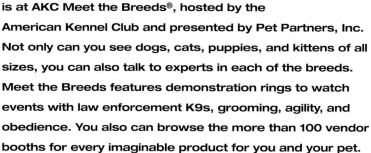

A great place to see Golden Retrievers and more than 200 other dog and cat breeds is at AKC Meet the Breeds®, hosted by the American Kennel Club and presented by Pet Partners, Inc. Not only can you see dogs, cats, puppies, and kittens of all sizes, you can also talk to experts in each of the breeds. Meet the Breeds features demonstration rings to watch events with law enforcement K9s, grooming, agility, and obedience. You also can browse the more than 100 vendor booths for every imaginable product for you and your pet.

It's great fun for the whole family. Meet the Breeds takes place in the fall in New York City. For more information, check out www.meetthebreeds.com.

STOP

WITHERS

BACK

MUZZLE

CHEST

BRISKET

ELBOW

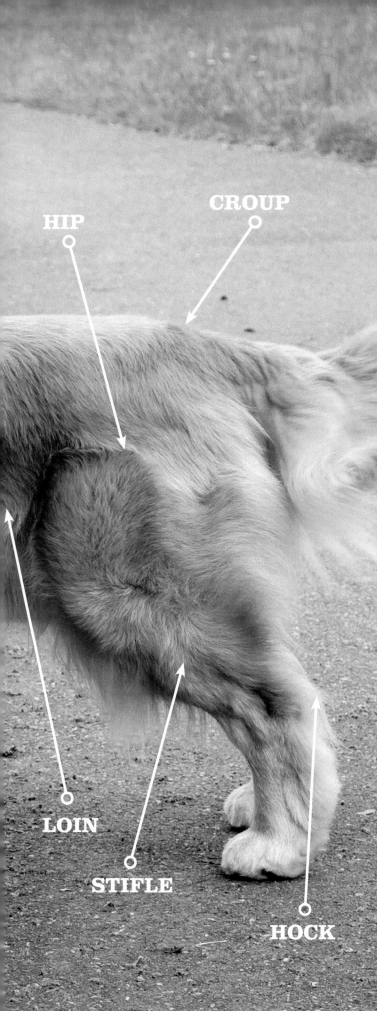

HIP

CROUP

LOIN

STIFLE

HOCK

The Golden in Brief

COUNTRY OF ORIGIN:
Scotland

ORIGINAL PURPOSE:
Hunting upland waterfowl

AVERAGE LIFE SPAN:
10 to 12 years

COAT:
Firm and resilient, dense and water-proof with a good undercoat; close-lying to the body, neither coarse nor silky; may be straight or wavy.

COLOR:
Any shade of a lustrous golden; white markings are frowned upon, except when due to aging. Goldens should neither be white nor Irish Setter red.

GROOMING:
Regular grooming is required to keep the Golden's full coat shiny and healthy. Two annual shedding periods are very heavy, during which time daily grooming is recommended.

HEIGHT/WEIGHT:
Males: 23-24 inches at the shoulder; 65-75 pounds. Females: 21½-22½ inches; 55-65 pounds.

TRAINABILITY:
Boundless

PERSONALITY:
Abundantly friendly, happy, family-oriented; reliable and trustworthy; smiling, tail-wagging, fun on four legs.

ACTIVITY LEVEL:
Very high

GOOD WITH OTHER PETS:
Yes, with proper introductions

NATIONAL BREED CLUB:
Golden Retriever Club of America; www.grca.org

RESCUE:
Golden Retriever Club of America National Rescue Committee; http://grca-nrc.org

A Golden Retriever definitely lives up to his Sporting dog ancestry. He must be lean, well structured, and eager for both work and play.

(shoulders) and females 21½ to 22½ inches. Ideal weight for male Golden Retrievers range from 65 to 75 pounds; females, 55 to 65 pounds. Today, you might see Goldens several inches taller than the standard and weigh in excess of 90 pounds. In a Sporting dog, bigger is not better. Oversized dogs are not good representations of the breed, and a poorly structured dog would be unable to spend the day afield running and retrieving upland game and waterfowl. Even though your

Join the GRCA

The parent club of a canine breed is considered the expert on everything related to that breed of dog. It's responsible for safeguarding and promoting a particular dog breed. These national organizations are members of the American Kennel Club and are made up of knowledgeable breeders. Each parent club determines the breed standard, a written description of the most desired traits of an ideal specimen of the breed, which the AKC then officially approves. The standard is used for breeding practices and competition judging. The parent club of the Golden Retriever is the Golden Retriever Club of America (GRCA). Learn more about the club at its website, www.grca.org.

pet Golden's only interaction with a waterfowl may be his duck-and-sweet-potato stew, you still want your Golden to look and act like a proper Golden Retriever.

As seen at most dog shows, the Golden Retriever's coat is one of this breed's crowning glories. The standard describes it as "dense and water-repellent with good undercoat." That description is not about glamour, it's about utility. A working retriever needs a quality coat to protect him in the water. The coat may be straight or wavy and is neither coarse nor silky. The ruff on the dog's neck is never trimmed, again, in keeping with the dog's natural appearance.

What You Get

The Golden must be friendly. The standard refers to the correct expression as "friendly and intelligent." "Friendly" is also mentioned in the section on temperament: "Friendly, reliable, and trustworthy. Quarrelsomeness or hostility toward

Golden Retriever Foundation

The Golden Retriever Club of America is very proud of the Golden Retriever Foundation (GRF), www.golden retrieverfoundation.org, a non-profit organization that was established in 1997 to fund grants for Golden health research, rescue, and owner education after receiving a generous bequest from Golden owner Carol Buckman. Through careful management of tax-deductible donations from owners who love their dogs, the GRF has provided over $1 million toward health research, in partnership with the Morris Animal Foundation and the AKC Canine Health Foundation. This research is already providing benefits to help Goldens live longer, healthier lives.

The Golden Retriever Breed Standard

AMERICAN
KENNEL CLUB

GENERAL APPEARANCE: A symmetrical, powerful, active dog, sound and well put together, not clumsy nor long in the leg, displaying a kindly expression and possessing a personality that is eager, alert and self-confident.

SIZE, PROPORTION, SUBSTANCE

Males 23-24 inches in height at withers; females 21½-22½ inches. . . . Length from breastbone to point of buttocks slightly greater than height at withers in ratio of 12:11. Weight for males 65-75 pounds; females 55-65 pounds.

HEAD

Broad in skull, slightly arched laterally and longitudinally without prominence of frontal bones (forehead) or occipital bones. Stop well defined but not abrupt. . . . Eyes friendly and intelligent in expression, medium large with dark, close-fitting rims, set well apart and reasonably deep in sockets. Color preferably dark brown. . . . Ears rather short with front edge attached well behind and just above the eye and falling close to cheek. When pulled forward, tip of ear should just cover the eye. . . . Nose black or brownish black, though fading to a lighter shade in cold weather not serious.

NECKLINE, TOPLINE, BODY

Neck medium long, merging gradually into well laid back shoulders, giving sturdy, muscular appearance. No throatiness. Backline strong and level from withers to slightly sloping croup, whether standing or moving. . . . Tail well set on, thick and muscular at the base, following the natural line of the croup. . . . Carried with merry action, level or with some moderate upward curve; never curled over back nor between legs.

FOREQUARTERS

Muscular, well coordinated with hindquarters and capable of free movement. . . . Legs, viewed from the

front, straight with good bone, but not to the point of coarseness. . . . Feet medium size, round, compact, and well knuckled, with thick pads. Excess hair may be trimmed to show natural size and contour.

HINDQUARTERS

Broad and strongly muscled. Profile of croup slopes slightly; the pelvic bone slopes at a slightly greater angle (approximately 30 degrees from horizontal). In a natural stance, the femur joins the pelvis at approximately a 90-degree angle; stifles well bent; hocks well let down with short, strong rear pasterns.

COAT

Dense and water-repellent with good undercoat. Outer coat firm and resilient, neither coarse nor silky, lying close to body; may be straight or wavy. Untrimmed natural ruff; moderate feathering on back of forelegs and on underbody; heavier feathering on front of neck, back of thighs and underside of tail.

COLOR

Rich, lustrous golden of various shades. Feathering may be lighter than rest of coat. . . . Predominant body color which is either extremely pale or extremely dark is undesirable.

GAIT

When trotting, gait is free, smooth, powerful and well coordinated, showing good reach. . . . As speed increases, feet tend to converge toward center line of balance. It is recommended that dogs be shown on a loose lead to reflect true gait.

—Excerpts from the American Kennel Club Breed Standard

*For the complete standard, visit www.grca.org

other dogs or people in normal situations, or an unwarranted show of timidity or nervousness, is not in keeping with Golden Retriever character." The Golden's characteristic love-everyone affability might be the breed's most defining quality. Goldens that are unpredictably hostile or nasty are not typical of the breed (or any breed!) and should not be bred and should be avoided by puppy buyers.

LEARNING MORE

If you are still in love with the Golden Retriever after everything you've learned, the next step is to meet and talk with other Golden Retriever owners about their personal experiences with their dogs. The best way to do this is to get in touch with your local breed club, which you can locate through the Golden Retriever Club of America's website, www.grca.org, or through the American Kennel Club's website, www.akc.org. You can also attend local dog shows where you can meet Goldens and talk with their owners and breeders. Hearing stories about the breed directly from owners and breeders will provide useful information as you begin the search for your own Golden Retriever puppy.

Goldens' affable, loving personalities are so recognized and cherished that temperament is a large part of the breed's official breed standard.

At a Glance ...

The Golden Retriever belongs to the AKC Sporting Group. Retrievers are bred for hunting and retrieving waterfowl, and regardless of whether or not you use your Golden to hunt, this "need to retrieve" is in his blood. Your Golden will love to play a rousing game of fetch and will retrieve anything for you, from slippers to newspapers to Frisbees.

Goldens are considered large dogs, ranging from 21 to 24 inches in height and weighing anywhere from 55 to 75 pounds. A Golden requires lots of exercise, training, and a lot of open space to run and play freely.

The Golden Retriever's signature golden coat requires daily brushing to keep shedding to a minimum. Nevertheless, a Golden owner can expect a significant amount of fur around the house. Keep this in mind when deciding whether a Golden is right for you—and keep your vacuum handy!

CHAPTER THREE

The Search for Gold

Because there seems to be a Golden Retriever in every neighborhood in the country, you may think that it shouldn't be too hard to find a litter of great Goldens. This is far from the truth. You must look for a reputable breeder who is breeding the kind of dog you have your heart set on. Most prospective owners know exactly why they want a Golden Retriever: a family pet, a jogging companion, a show dog, a weekend hunting dog, or possibly a competition

Golden Retrievers come in a range of various golden shades. Often, puppies are born with lighter coloring, but their color should deepen as they grow older.

dog for obedience, agility, or field trials. Maybe they want to help the community by being part of a therapy dog team with their Golden or train for search and rescue. With so much versatility in the breed, it's wise to choose a breeder who produces dogs that have done the things you're looking to do.

THE RIGHT CHOICE

Beyond these considerations, what's most important is the health of a breeder's dogs. Most purebred dogs have health problems that breeders keep an eye on when planning a litter. Conscientious breeders screen their stock for certain health issues. The Golden Retriever Club of America recommends screening for four health concerns common in the breed: hip dysplasia, elbow dysplasia, eye disorders, and hereditary heart disease. Visit www.grca.org for more information about these and other health matters. Find a breeder you can trust, who has experience with the breed, screens his or her potential sires (fathers) and dams (mothers) for genetic disorders, raises healthy and sound puppies, and can provide documentation of his or her dogs' health. It will take time, but a friendly, healthy, beautiful pup is worth the extra effort and, yes, the price.

Most people are very anxious to get a puppy once they have decided which breed they want. It's critical to be patient, and think with your head and not your heart. A puppy search can be an emotionally trying experience, taxing your patience and will power. All puppies are adorable and instantly lovable. Don't fall for the first ball of golden puppy fur you see. Do your breeder homework before you visit the kennel and the pups. Arm yourself with a list of questions for the breeder. Leave your wallet and your kids at home so you aren't tempted to take home a poorly bred but nonetheless irresistible Golden pup.

COMMON QUESTIONS FOR OWNERS

Meeting a breeder often begins with a Q&A session. The breeder will have many questions for you, and you should have questions for the breeder as well. Be prepared to answer any and all of the following questions:

- Have you owned a dog before? If yes, which breeds?
- What became of your previous dog or dogs?
- What sort of home do you live in? An apartment or condo, a house with a yard? Does the yard have a fence?
- Do you have children? If yes, what ages? What kind of exposure have the children had to dogs?
- Does everyone in the household want a new dog? Does anyone have allergies to dogs?
- Do you work full time? Is anyone in the home during the day? Can you make arrangements for doggy day care or a dog walker?
- What are your hopes for the dog's education? Basic training, obedience, showing, hunting, etc.?

The breeder's primary concern is the future of his or her puppies and whether you and your family are suitable owners who will provide a proper and loving home for one of his or her progeny for the dog's entire life. In short, the breeder hopes that you have had experience with dogs; took care of any previously owned dogs for their full lives and trained them responsibly; have well-behaved children, regardless of their age; can look after the dog during the day; and have some idea what you want to do with the dog. Most breeders know that pet owners aren't going to show their dogs or pursue a career in obedience trials, though training the dog sufficiently that he can pass the Canine Good Citizen® test is perfectly within the sights of every Golden Retriever owner.

Be suspicious of any breeder who agrees to sell you a Golden Retriever puppy without any interview process at all. This lack of concern about his or her pups

Did You Know?

The Golden Retriever is one of six retrievers in the Sporting Group. The most popular, of course, is the Labrador Retriever. Two other British retrievers, named for their coats, are the Flat-Coated and the Curly-Coated Retrievers. The other two retrievers hail from North America, the Nova Scotia Duck Tolling Retriever, proudly claimed by Canada, and the Chesapeake Bay Retriever, a USA original from Maryland. The Sporting Group contains twenty-eight breeds and also includes Pointers, Spaniels, and Setters.

Golden Retrievers are great family pets, but selecting the right puppy is a decision for adults. Consult your breeder and trust his or her judgment on matching you and your family with the perfect puppy.

casts doubt on the breeder's ethics and breeding program. It's time to leave if the breeder's only question is: "Visa or Mastercard?"

QUESTIONS FOR THE BREEDER

You will also have a chance to learn more about your breeder by asking questions of your own. Your breeder should be more than willing to answer any and all questions that you may have about his or her breeding practices and about Golden Retrievers in general. Here are some questions that you should consider asking the breeder:

Why did you plan this breeding?

A conscientious breeder plans a litter of Golden Retriever puppies for specific reasons and should be able to explain why he or she paired this particular male and female and what he or she expects the breeding to produce. The breeder may be honest enough to say, "I had over a dozen people on my puppy buyer's list and needed to breed some puppies to sell." That's not necessarily a bad thing. In fact, a breeder with a waiting list is a good thing because it shows that his or her dogs are in demand. What you don't want to hear is that the breeder simply wanted to see what his or her dog and the neighbor's dog would come up with or that he or she wanted to let the kids experience "the miracle of birth."

Who are the parents of the litter and have they both been screened for common Golden Retriever health problems?

Both the mother and the father should be at least two years old before being bred. The dam of the litter should be on the breeder's premises. The sire may be owned by a different breeder and may not be present. If neither parent is available to see, you should be concerned. Regarding health screening, responsible breeders, especially those who belong to the parent club, will screen their dogs for the "big four": heart disorders, hip and elbow dysplasia, and eye problems. Breeders should be forthcoming about the results of their screenings and should provide a copy of the health screening reports. Do not accept the breeder at his or her word alone. You do not want to hear a breeder say, "She doesn't have the best elbows or hips, but she has the prettiest head and nicest temperament I've ever seen," or even worse,

Get Your Registration and Pedigree

A responsible breeder will be able to provide your family with an American Kennel Club registration form and pedigree.

AKC REGISTRATION: When you buy a Golden Retriever from a breeder, ask the breeder for an American Kennel Club Dog Registration Application form. The breeder will fill out most of the application for you. When you fill out your portion of the document and mail it to the AKC, you will receive a Registration Certificate proving that your dog is officially part of the AKC. Besides recording your name and your dog's name in the AKC database, registration helps fund the AKC's good works such as canine health research, search-and-rescue teams, educating the public about responsible dog care, and much more.

CERTIFIED PEDIGREE: A pedigree is an AKC certificate proving that your dog is a purebred. It shows your puppy's family tree, listing the names of his parents and grandparents. If your dog is registered with the AKC, the organization will have a copy of your dog's pedigree on file, which you can order from its website (www.akc.org). Look for any titles that your Golden's ancestors have won, including Champion (conformation), Companion Dog (obedience), Tracking Dog (tracking), and so forth. A pedigree doesn't guarantee the health or personality of a dog, but it's a starting point for picking out a good Golden puppy.

"There's no need to screen my dogs due to their purebred ancestry." Also, be sure to ask about the history of cancer in the breeder's dogs. This is a major health concern in Golden Retrievers. Good health and soundness are the most important considerations, but don't sacrifice temperament for good elbows. It's perfectly reasonable to expect good elbows on a healthy, friendly dog!

How long have you been involved in dogs (or Goldens in specific)?

Experienced Golden Retriever breeders are frequently involved in some aspect of the dog fancy with their dogs, perhaps showing in conformation, competing in hunt tests or field trials, or training for other performance events or dog-related activities. Dedicated breeders often belong to the Golden Retriever Club of America (GRCA) and a local breed or kennel club, and they may be AKC Breeders of Merit. Such affiliation expands their knowledge of their chosen breed, which further enhances their credibility. Most breeders stay in the breed for an average of six to ten years, which is ample time to earn a championship on a dog or performance titles. If the breeder has no interest in AKC events, this is a red flag.

When you visit a breeder, ask to see the parents of the litter. Temperament is inherited, so be sure that the mother is friendly and outgoing—traits you want in your future puppy.

Why Should You Register with the American Kennel Club?

Registering your puppy with the American Kennel Club does more than just certify the lineage of your Golden Retriever. It helps the AKC do many good things for dogs everywhere, such as promote responsible breeding and support the care and health of dogs throughout the world. As a result of your registration, the AKC is able to inspect kennels across the country, educate dog owners about the importance of training through the Canine Good Citizen® Program, support search-and-rescue canines via the AKC Companion Animal Recovery Canine Support and Relief Fund, teach the public about the importance of responsible dog ownership through publications and the annual AKC Responsible Dog Ownership Days, and much more. Not only is the AKC a respected organization dedicated to the registration of purebred dogs, but it is also devoted to the well-being of dogs everywhere. For more information, go to www.akc.org/reg.

What kind of guarantees do you offer on your puppies?

Reputable breeders have a puppy sales contract that includes specific health guarantees and reasonable return policies. Never buy a dog without a contract that specifies the responsibilities of the breeder and the buyer. The breeder should always agree to accept the puppy back if things do not work out. He or she also should be willing, indeed anxious, to check up on the puppy's progress and be available if you have questions or problems with the pup.

Can you provide me with any references?

Feel free to ask for references and check with them. It's unlikely that a breeder will offer names of unhappy puppy clients, but calling other owners may make you more comfortable dealing with that particular breeder. Of course, a good reference in itself is that the breeder is a GRCA member. Member breeders can be found listed on the club's website at www.grca.org.

THE PERFECT PUPPY

A reputable breeder is the key to picking the right puppy. The breeder's experience with the breed is invaluable in helping you select your Golden puppy. A good breeder has experience with the Golden Retriever, understands the health and genetic issues that affect the breed, and selects breeding stock with care. The breeder also evaluates the puppies and helps clients find the pup that will best suit their needs and lifestyle.

The Price You Pay

In difficult economic times, everyone is looking for a bargain. You may think finding a cheap Golden puppy through the local newspaper or online may be all your current budget will allow. Think again! The GRCA reminds potential owners, "Your puppy's purchase price may be a smidgen of what you spend over its lifetime." This is sound advice considering how much money you can spend on veterinary bills over the course of your Golden's life. Choosing a puppy from a conscientious breeder who has socialized the pups and screened the parents for common health issues makes the most sense, emotionally and financially. Expect to pay a reasonable price for a sound, healthy, typical Golden puppy.

The perfect puppy is seldom right around the corner. Be willing to travel to visit any litter of pups you are considering and, if possible, visit more than one. You will be surprised at the difference from one breeder and litter to the next. You'll be a smarter shopper for your efforts and will end up with a better pup. If you visit more than one breeder, go home in between visits and shower and change clothes, including your shoes. It's easy to pick up germs and parasites from a kennel and transfer them to other susceptible young puppies.

A puppy visit is like the ultimate job interview, so be ready. While searching for your new Golden, check out all the applicants—the puppies, their parents, and the breeder, as well as the living environment in which the pups are raised.

Where and how a litter of pups is raised has a big impact on how the puppies develop into confident, well-socialized adults. The litter should be kept in the breeder's house or in an adjoining sheltered area. Some breeders have a separate kennel building to house their dogs and puppies. You will know that you have found an exceptional breeder when you see the walls lined with photographs of dogs in the show ring, blue ribbons, and dozens of champion certificates.

Whether raised in the home or in a clean kennel, all Golden Retriever puppies need to be socialized daily with people and human activities. The greater the pups' exposure to household sights and sounds between four and eight weeks of age, the easier their adjustment will be to their future human family.

During your visit, scrutinize the puppies and their living area for cleanliness and signs of compromised health. The pups should be reasonably clean, though puppies at this age are nonstop poop machines. They should appear energetic, bright-eyed, and alert. Healthy pups have clean, thick coats, are well proportioned, and feel solid and muscular without being overly fat or pot-bellied. A

Who Should Choose a Different Breed?

Anyone seeking a watchdog or guard dog. Goldens welcome intruders and their bark always says, "How you doing, mister? Come over and play with me!"

Anyone who is house-fussy or lives with someone who's super fastidious. Goldens love water, but they love puddles and mud even more. And, they shed twelve months a year.

Anyone who's looking for a one-man dog. Your Golden will surely love you, but he'll love everyone in the household, the neighborhood, the town, and the nearby towns, too.

Anyone who's never home. Goldens love to have their people near them. They'll just as happily run on a beach with you as sleep next to you on the couch. As long as they're near you, they're happy.

Anyone who's a boring couch potato. Lazy folk ain't Golden folk. Goldens thrive when they're out and about, doing fun stuff with the people they love.

distended belly may be a sign of intestinal parasites. Check for evidence of watery or bloody stools. Watch for crusted eyes or noses or any watery discharge from the noses, eyes, or ears. Listen for coughing or excessive sniffing and snorting.

Visit with the litter's mother and also the father, if possible. In many cases the father is not on the premises, but the breeder should have photos of the father, his pedigree, and a résumé of his characteristics, health clearances, and accomplishments. It is normal for some dams to be somewhat protective of their young, but overly aggressive behavior is unacceptable. Temperament is inherited, and if one or both parents are aggressive or very shy, it is likely that some of the pups will inherit those atypical and undesirable characteristics.

Notice how the pups interact with their littermates and their surroundings, especially their responses to people. They should be active and outgoing. In most Golden litters, some pups will be more outgoing than others, but even a quiet puppy that is properly socialized should not be shy or shrink from a friendly voice or outstretched hand.

The breeder has spent the most time cuddling and cleaning up after the puppies, and he or she knows the subtle differences in each pup's personality. The breeder should be honest in discussing any differences in the puppies' personalities and will help you select the Golden puppy that is right for you. Tell the breeder if you plan to show your pup, hunt, or compete in sporting activities. Some puppies will show more promise than others, and the breeder can help you select one that will best suit your lifestyle and long-term goals.

BLUE OR PINK?

Have you already decided if you want a boy or a girl puppy? Both are loving and loyal, and the differences are due more to individual personalities than to sex. The adult Golden Retriever female is a lovable girl and easy to live with, but she also can be a bit moody, depending on her whims and hormonal peaks. The adult

If you visit more than one breeder in one day, be sure to shower and change clothes in between visits, including your shoes. You don't want to transfer any illnesses or parasites from one kennel to another.

male is often up to 2 inches taller than the female and is heavier boned, weighing 65 to 75 pounds. Although males tend to be more even-tempered than females, they are also more physical and exuberant during adolescence, which can be a handful with such a large and energetic dog. An untrained male can also become dominant with people and other dogs. A solid foundation in obedience is necessary if you want your Golden pup to respect you as his leader.

If you are interested in showing your dog, he or she must remain intact. The conformation sport is based on choosing the best dogs for breeding purposes to produce puppies in line with the breed standard. If you are not planning on showing your dog, consider spaying or neutering your pet. The spay/neuter process, advised for all "pet-only" dogs, creates a level playing field and eliminates most sex differences. Your Golden Retriever may live longer, too, as spaying or neutering lowers the risk of some female uterine conditions and several forms of cancer.

NECESSARY PAPERWORK

Once you choose a puppy, the breeder will let you know when you can take him home—usually when he is eight to twelve weeks old. At that time, your breeder will also give you a packet of paperwork to read and sign. Be sure that these documents include a puppy sales contract, pedigree and registration papers, and the puppy's health records and vaccination history. Some breeders will also include a general care kit with information on the breed, a sample of food that the breeder has been feeding the puppies, and a small blanket with the scent of the puppy's mother and littermates to help in your pup's transition to a new home.

Contract: Reputable breeders will have a puppy sales contract that outlines the puppy's cost, health guarantees, and reasonable return policies. It will also include any spay/neuter requirements that the breeder may require if you will not be showing your dog.

Pedigree and registration papers: When you purchase your puppy, your breeder should provide you with a partially filled-out AKC Dog Registration Application. Your breeder should also provide a detailed pedigree, or family tree, showing your Golden's parentage going back several generations. Once you get home, fill out the registration application completely and mail it to the American Kennel Club. Within a few weeks, you will receive a Registration Certificate.

Health records: Your breeder will give you an assortment of documentation ensuring the health and temperament of your puppy. A complete history of your puppy's date of birth and medical records should be included, which will list any vaccinations, temperament testing, or procedures that your puppy has received or undergone. You should also receive a copy of the temperament and health testing documentation of the puppy's mother and father.

Take your time when looking for a puppy. Visit a few different litters, and interact with many different puppies. A good breeder will help you pick the right Golden Retriever pup for your lifestyle.

THE LAST WORD

By the time they are ready to leave the breeder, the Golden Retriever puppies should have had at least one worming, their first puppy shots, and a veterinarian exam verifying their good health. The breeder should also tell you what the pup has been eating, when, and how much.

Many breeders will also supply literature on the breed and books or pamphlets on how to properly raise a Golden Retriever pup. Dedicated breeders know that the more you know, the better the life ahead for their precious Golden pups. Your goal should be to find one of those breeders.

Your breeder will be an asset to you throughout your dog's life. Don't hesitate to call your breeder for advice—your breeder should be happy to help.

At a Glance ...

Finding a responsible breeder can be a daunting task, especially for a breed as popular as the Golden Retriever. Contact the Golden Retriever Club of America (www.grca.org) or your local breed club to help you find a responsible breeder in your area.

Don't fall in love with the first pair of puppy-dog eyes you see! Take the time to visit a few different litters of puppies and examine each pup from nose to tail. Healthy puppies should have clean eyes, ears, noses, and bottoms, with outgoing, friendly personalities to match.

Be sure to get all the paperwork you'll need from your breeder at the time of your puppy's purchase. Responsible breeders will create a packet for you that should include the puppy's sales contract, health certificate, vaccination records, pedigree, registration form, and any other materials that your breeder feels will help your puppy's transition to his new home.

CHAPTER FOUR

A Golden Homecoming

Whether this Golden Retriever puppy is your first or your tenth, homecoming is always exciting. Introducing a new friend to your world can go very smoothly with a little advanced planning. Make your puppy's transition to his new home a safe and happy one. Before you bring your puppy home, stock up on supplies and puppy-proof to make sure your home is safe for your puppy (and your house is safe from the pup!).

The first twenty weeks of your puppy's life is a very important time for socialization. Introduce your pup to a variety of new situations and people for him to learn and grow.

STOCKING UP FOR YOUR GOLDEN

Shopping for puppy supplies is fun, and a pet superstore or well-stocked pet shop is the ideal one-stop outlet you need. In addition to the items listed below, you'll be tempted by the array of dog products available. Some essentials you will need right away include food bowls, food, a collar and leash, and a crate. You don't need to fill your puppy's toy box in one day; so take your time and shop wisely.

Food and Water Bowls

You'll need two separate serving dishes, one for food and one for water. Stainless steel bowls are your best choice, as they are lightweight, chew-proof, and easy to clean. Tip-proof is a good idea, too, because most Golden Retriever puppies love to splash around in their water bowls. You may also want to purchase an additional stainless steel water bowl or bucket to put outdoors.

Puppy Food

Your Golden Retriever puppy should be fed a quality food that is appropriate for his age and breed. Many dog foods now are offered in specific formulas that address the nutritional needs of small, medium, and large (your Golden) breeds of dog during the various stages of their lives. Large-breed puppy food, formulated to promote healthy growth, should be your dog's diet for the first year. After that, you can switch to a large-breed adult-maintenance food.

Your Golden's early growth period as well as his long-term health will benefit from a diet of high-quality puppy and dog food. For good recommendations, check with your breeder and your veterinarian before you choose your puppy's food. You may want to stick with the food that the breeder fed, especially if your puppy eats it with gusto.

For more information about feeding your Golden Retriever, see chapter 8.

Collars and ID Tags

Your Golden Retriever pup should have an adjustable collar that expands to fit him as he grows. Lightweight nylon adjustable collars work best for both puppies and adult dogs. Put the collar on as soon as your puppy comes home so he can get used to wearing it. The ID tag should have your phone number, name, and address. Attach the tag with an "O" ring (similar to key rings), as the more common "S" ring snags on carpets and comes off easily.

Some high-tech dog collars come equipped with beepers and tracking devices. The most advanced pet-identification tool uses a Global Positioning System (GPS) and fits inside a collar or tag. When your dog leaves his programmed home perimeter, the device sends a message directly to your phone or e-mail address.

Nylon choke collars are for training purposes and should be worn only during training sessions. Training collars should never be used on Golden Retriever puppies under sixteen weeks of age, and do not use a collar that may pull or damage his coat. Metal collars, for instance, are not recommended for coated breeds like the Golden.

Your puppy may not look like he requires a lot, but there are a few essentials that he needs right away, such as food, food bowls, a collar and leash, a crate, and a few toys.

Leashes

For your puppy's safety and your convenience, purchase two kinds of leashes. A narrow six-foot leather or nylon leash is best for walks, puppy kindergarten, obedience classes, and leash training.

A PIECE OF HISTORY

In the early 1900s, Golden Retrievers were known as Flat Coats (Golden). In 1911, they were recognized as a new breed called a Retriever, of which there were many different varieties. It wasn't until 1933 that the breed's name was officially changed to Golden Retriever and recognized as a separate breed.

The other leash is a flexible one that is housed in a large handle, that extends and retracts with the push of a button. This is the ideal tool for exercising puppies and adult dogs and should be a staple for every Golden once he behaves well on a regular leash. Extendable leashes are available in several lengths (up to 26 feet) and strengths, depending on breed size. Longer is better, as it allows your dog to run about and check out the good sniffing areas farther away from you. They are especially handy for exercising your puppy in unfenced areas or when traveling with your dog.

Bedding

You can really overdo it when it comes to dog beds! Beds run the gamut from basic and inexpensive to over-the-top and elaborate. Keep in mind that the fun-loving, energetic Golden won't spend too much time in a canopy bed with ruffled pillows.

Think Outside the Box

Many potential dog owners are discouraged by the 24/7 demands of a puppy or a young dog. People who work full-time or have other time-consuming obligations often feel that they are not ideal dog owners. Here are some suggestions and options for dog owners who have time constraints:

Doggy Day Care: Professional, reliable centers have sprung up in cities and towns around the country. They provide daily playtime, exercise, and socialization for puppies and dogs alike. Goldens are social dogs and make ideal candidates for day care.

Dog Walkers and Sitters: Owners can hire certified professionals to stop by your home and walk your dog or spend an hour playing with him in the backyard. Knowing that the dog gets a mid-day break and a light lunch can make all the difference in the world to a concerned owner who's unable to get home from work.

Second Dog: Two dogs is not much more work than one. Walking and feeding a second dog doesn't add much time to an owner's schedule. The second dog in the house can provide company for your dog when you're away from home. Goldens love other dogs and always welcome a friend into their homes.

Neighbors, Family, and Friends: Perhaps someone in your life loves dogs and would be happy to visit your dog on a regular basis. Offering them some incentive—money, a favor, professional assistance— can also persuade people to pitch in.

Your Golden Retriever puppy is more likely to wet and shred a fancy bed than sleep in it, so you're wiser to use a large towel, mat, or blanket that can be easily laundered. Once your dog is reliably house-trained and sufficiently over his teething phase, invest in a nice full-size bed that your dog will be comfortable napping on.

Crates, Gates, and Pens

A crate, a series of baby gates, or exercise pens/enclosures will be your most important puppy purchases. A crate is a valuable tool for house-training your puppy and his favorite place to feel secure. Crates come in three varieties: wire, fabric mesh, and plastic. Wire- or fabric-mesh crates offer the best ventilation, and some conveniently fold up. A fabric-mesh crate might be a little risky for a Golden youngster that likes to dig and chew. A plastic airline-type crate is more sturdy, and it offers a more private, den-like environment for your dog. Plastic crates are bulky, but they are durable and great for travel.

Whatever your choice, purchase an adult-sized crate that your Golden will grow into. While your puppy is small, use a divider to block off the back of the crate, in other words, fit the size of the crate to your puppy. Dogs are clean by nature, and they instinctually do not like to soil their sleeping areas. This is what makes a crate so useful in house-training. However, if the crate is too large, your puppy may be tempted to go to the bathroom at one end of the crate and sleep in the other. By using a divider, you can invest in an adult crate, but slowly grow the interior space as your puppy gets older.

Well-placed, sturdy baby gates will protect your house from potential damage from your new puppy. Gates also teach the puppy structure and discipline.

Common Household Poisons

Many items that you use every day in your home and yard can be toxic to dogs. They can cause rashes, vomiting, diarrhea, or worse. As you're puppy-proofing your home, put these products out of your dog's reach.

- Acetaminophen
- Antifreeze
- Bleach
- Boric acid
- Car fluids
- Cleaning fluids
- Deodorizers
- Detergents
- Disinfectants
- Drain cleaners
- Furniture polish
- Gasoline
- Herbicides
- Insecticides
- Kerosene
- Matches
- Mothballs
- Nail polish and remover
- Paint
- Prescription medication
- Rat poison
- Rubbing alcohol
- Snail or slug bait
- Turpentine

Confine your puppy to a tiled or uncarpeted room or space, one that is easily cleaned and accessible to the outside door he will use for potty trips. In most homes, that's the kitchen. Gated to a safe area where he cannot chew valuable furniture or soil carpeting, the puppy will soon master house-training, chew only appropriate chew toys, and spare you and himself from unnecessary corrections for normal puppy mishaps.

Exercise pens consist of several wire panels that can be set up to confine your puppy in a specific area of the house. Similar to a child's playpen, put your dog's crate, a few toys, and some newspaper (for relieving himself) in the pen to keep your Golden entertained when you can't keep an eye on him.

Remember, gated or penned does not mean unsupervised. Golden puppies bore easily and have been known to entertain themselves by chewing through things like doors and drywall. If your puppy must be unattended, use his crate.

Brushes and Grooming Tools

A soft bristle brush of any kind works well on a young Golden's coat. Once his adult coat starts to come in, which is a bit coarser than puppy fur, you will need a pin brush and a slicker brush for routine grooming; a steel comb called a "Greyhound comb," which has wide- and narrow-spaced teeth; and a mat rake and shedding comb,

both excellent tools for periods of heavy shedding. Ask your breeder or groomer for recommendations.

Introduce your puppy to brushing early on so he learns to like the process. You want your dog to look forward to grooming time because you will be grooming him all the time. Grooming also helps condition the pup to hands-on attention, which will be invaluable when you have to brush his teeth, clean his ears, and clip his nails.

Toys

Retriever puppies love toys that they can mouth, fetch, and carry around. Many pups will snuggle with their fuzzy stuffed friends as they would their littermates. Eventually most puppies will destroy soft or fuzzy toys, which is your cue to remove and replace them.

Golden Retrievers love anything they can retrieve, so keep this in mind when selecting your pup's first toys. Safe chew toys are a must if you hope to direct your Golden's chewing to acceptable objects and away from your shoes and other possessions. Nylon or hard sterilized bones are excellent pacifiers and come in age-appropriate sizes.

Hard rubber toys are fine, but avoid soft, flexible plastic or any toys with parts or squeakers that could be swallowed. One important puppy toy rule: offer only a couple of toys at a time, and rotate them every other day. If you give your puppy a full toy box of stuff, he may be overwhelmed and become bored with all of them.

DON'T FORGET TO PUPPY-PROOF

You'll be amazed at the objects your Golden Retriever puppy finds to chew on, dig up, and destroy. Your Golden is clever. Match that with a high-energy need to

Your Golden Retriever will chew anything he can get his paws on, including your favorite dress shoes! Redirect your dog's chewing habits to appropriate chew toys such as hard rubber toys or nylon bones.

Consider the Microchip

In addition to a dog collar and ID tag, think about having your veterinarian insert a microchip in your dog to help find him if he ever gets lost. When scanned, the microchip will show your dog's unique microchip number so that your Golden Retriever can be returned to you as soon as possible. Go to www.akccar.org to learn more about the nonprofit American Kennel Club Companion Animal Recovery (AKC CAR) pet recovery system.

Since 1995, the AKC CAR recovery service has been selected by millions of dog owners who are grateful for the peace of mind and service that AKC CAR offers. Learn more at www.akccar.org.

AMERICAN KENNEL CLUB

A Golden that has been socialized from puppyhood can grow up to be a reliable companion, therapy dog, or even a service dog.

retrieve and an insatiable need to chew, and you have a very probable puppy tornado on your hands. Be proactive and puppy-proof your home before you bring your Golden home. Even though you won't be letting your puppy out of your sight any time soon, it's best to put all breakable and irreplaceable objects out of reach and out of sight just to be safe.

The best way to start puppy-proofing is to get down on your hands and knees and view the world from your puppy's perspective. You'll be surprised to learn that lamp wires and tablecloth edges are right at eye level, tempting a curious pup. Tuck away all loose cords under furniture, or hide them behind specially made plastic covers. Sharp puppy teeth can easily chew through electrical cords and cause serious injury to your Golden.

An array of delicious smells (to your dog at least) emanate from the kitchen garbage. Invest in a sturdy trash can with a sealable, tamper-proof lid. Start taking out the trash regularly so your Golden Retriever doesn't have the chance to dig through it. Gather all cleaning materials, dishwasher soaps, and other hazardous materials, and place them behind a locked cabinet or closed bathroom door. Be sure to close all toilet lids so that your Golden doesn't get into the habit of drinking from the bowl.

If your Golden will have access to the garage, put away all engine oils, fluids, and antifreeze. These are extremely toxic to your dog, and even a small amount can be fatal. Beware of sharp lawn mower blades, tools, and backyard pesticides. These also should be placed behind locked cabinet doors.

Your Golden Retriever is a veritable Houdini. Even after setting up baby gates, constructing barriers, closing doors, and installing child locks, you will realize that your determined Golden will still find something to get into. Make an effort to stay one step ahead of your pup. Use common sense and have patience, and you and your Golden will learn to live together safely and peacefully.

SOCIALIZATION

We use the term "socialization" to mean proactively exposing a puppy to the human world. Without question, puppy socialization can mean the difference between a well-adjusted, easygoing, people-happy dog and a shy, skittish dog. Although Goldens are outgoing and gregarious by nature, every dog is different, and owners should take nothing for granted. It's important to expose all puppies to everyday noises and household activities, outdoor places, strangers, and new situations at an early age.

Do You Need a License?

Some county and state laws require owners to apply for a license for their pets. Contact the nearest animal-control agency to find out if you need a license for your Golden Retriever. If a license is required, you will fill out an application, which includes your name, address, and phone number, as well as your pet's name, breed, sex, age, microchip number (if applicable), and whether your Golden has been spayed or neutered (a sterilization certificate). You also will have to show proof of your dog's rabies vaccination. You will receive a license tag to attach to your dog's collar. This will help animal-control officers find you if your dog becomes lost.

Let's Get Social

Dog people are always talking about "socialization." Whether they're breeders, trainers, or behaviorists, socialization has been a buzz word for generations. In order for puppies to grow up to be well adjusted, they need to meet people from all walks of life and experience various activities in new and different environments. Bring your puppy with you everywhere you go— the mall, a church bake sale, the park, a family party, even to your office, if that's possible. Puppies that miss out on social opportunities when they are young will likely not be as outgoing, comfortable, and well adjusted as puppies that know the joy of being the center of attention!

Unsocialized pups can grow up to be insecure and untrusting of people, children, and strange places. Many turn into fear biters or become aggressive with other dogs, strangers, and even people they know. It takes much time, effort, and patience to rehabilitate these dogs, and they often end up in animal shelters.

A dog's primary socialization period occurs during his first twenty weeks of life. Once he leaves the safety of his mother and littermates at eight to ten weeks of age, your job begins. Give your puppy a couple of quiet days to get used to his new home, then gradually introduce him to the sights and sounds of his new human world. Until your puppy has had all his vaccinations, restrict his interactions with other dogs, but feel free to introduce him to people. Frequent socialization with children, teens, adults, and seniors is essential at this age. Visit new places (dog-friendly, of course) like parks or even the local grocery-store or mall parking lot where there are crowds of people. A pet superstore that allows pets inside is always a great choice. Set a goal of two new places a week for the next two months. Keep these new situations upbeat and positive, and your pup will have a positive attitude toward future encounters and new experiences.

Your puppy will also need supervised exposure to children. Puppies of all breeds tend to view toddlers and small children as littermates and will attempt to exert the upper paw (a dominance ploy) over the child. Because he was bred to hunt and carry game, a Golden pup is very oral and will mouth a child's fingers and toes. Adult family members should supervise and teach the puppy not to nip at or jump on children.

Goldens are generally good with children, but their happy, bouncy ways could unintentionally overwhelm a small child during play. Both dog and child must be taught how to play properly with each other, and children must learn to handle the puppy with care and respect. Teach children not to entice the puppy into rambunctious behavior that could lead to a mishap.

Take full advantage of your young Golden pup's first few months in your home. The younger the puppy, the easier it is to instill good manners, desirable

habits, and reliable behavior patterns. A ten-week-old puppy has been described as a "blank slate" or an "empty sponge," ready to be marked by or absorb new experiences. Devote time to your puppy's education and socialization every day. Don't miss a single opportunity to expose your puppy to new people, places, and things and fill his "slate" or "sponge" with wonderful, positive experiences. A puppy that grows up to love life and the people around him gracefully matures into a well-adjusted adult dog that will be a pleasure to have around your home, your family, and your friends.

A sure sign of proper socialization: an irremovable Golden Retriever smile. Start socializing your Golden at a young age by introducing him to new people and new situations.

At a Glance ...

Purchase all your puppy necessities before bringing your Golden Retriever home. Food and water bowls, a leash, a collar, ID tags, grooming supplies, and a crate are some of the things you will need right away.

Your Golden Retriever is one smart and curious pup. Get down on all fours and view the world from his perspective, moving breakable objects out of reach and covering all electrical cords. Consider blocking off parts of the house at first until your Golden gets to know the house rules.

Socialization during the puppy's first three months in your home is the critical key to developing a well-adjusted adult Golden Retriever. Invite friends and family members over to visit your new puppy, and introduce him to a variety of new experiences and environments.

CHAPTER FIVE

Golden Rules

Intelligence comes natural to Golden Retrievers! After all, you didn't choose this breed just for its good looks. This purebred dog loves to learn and is easier to train than many other breeds. The key word here is "train." No breed, no matter how intelligent, is born pre-programmed to be mindful or obedient. Teaching your dog basic cues as well as house rules and good manners is your job, and this job starts the day you bring your puppy home.

Canines are pack animals by instinct. They're naturally communal and they rely on a leader to keep their pack orderly and effective. Your Golden Retriever's first leader was his mother, and all of his life lessons as a puppy were learned from his mom and littermates. When he played too rough or nipped too hard, his siblings cried and stopped the game. When he got pushy or obnoxious, his mother cuffed him gently with a maternal paw or gently shook him by the scruff of the neck. Now you have to assume the role of leader and communicate acceptable behavior in terms that his young canine mind will understand. Human rules make no sense to a dog, so you have to think like a dog!

The first five months of a dog's life are his most valuable learning time. His mind is best able to soak up every lesson—both positive and negative—at this young age. Positive experiences and proper socialization during this period are critical to his future development and stability. The amount and quality of time you invest with your Golden Retriever puppy now will determine what kind of an adult he will become. Wild or polite? Well behaved or naughty? It's up to you.

A GOLDEN BY ANY OTHER NAME

You may already have a name picked out for your Golden before you bring him home. Sometimes, though, it may take a week or two to discover the name that suits your new pup best. When deciding on a name for your dog, keep in mind that short, one- or two-syllable names are the easiest to use when training. Also, try not to choose a name that sounds like common training cues such as *sit*, *stay*, or *come*—in other words, reconsider names like Brit, Kay, or Krum (if you're a Harry Potter fan). This may confuse your Golden once you start more advanced obedience training.

Give your puppy plenty of exercise time before attempting to begin a lesson. He will be less energetic and more focused on your commands.

To help your Golden Retriever learn his name, call to him often. When he looks at you to see what the ruckus is about, toss him a treat. Do this multiple times a day, and after a few days, your Golden will start answering to his name with or without a treat as a reward.

THE BEST POLICY

Canine behavioral science tells us that any behavior that is rewarded will be repeated. It's called positive reinforcement. If something good happens, like a tasty treat or hugs and kisses, a puppy will naturally want to repeat the behavior. That same research also has proven that one of the best ways to a puppy's mind is through his stomach. Never underestimate the power of a treat!

The same reinforcement principle applies to behavior that we consider negative, like scavenging through the trash can, digging a hole in your garden, or chewing on your loafers. These are all behaviors that your puppy does not know is "wrong." If your dog gets into the garbage, steals food, or does anything else that he thinks is fun or makes him feel good, he will do it again. That's why it's so important to keep a sharp eye on your puppy so you can catch him in the act and teach him which behaviors are not acceptable.

PUPPY-TRAINING PRINCIPLES

Successful puppy training depends on several important principles:

1. Use simple one-word cues and say them only once. Otherwise, a puppy learns that "come" (or "sit" or "down") is a three- or four-word cue.

Did You Know?

The first three dogs to win an AKC Obedience Trial Champion (OTCH) title were Golden Retrievers. Though the obedience sport has its roots in the 1930s, the OTCH title was first awarded in 1977.

The first lesson to teach your Golden Retriever is his name. Call to your pup by saying his name, and when you have his attention, give him a treat. He'll learn his name in just a few days.

2. Never correct your dog for something he did minutes earlier. If it is more than three to five seconds after the fact, your dog will not understand what he is being corrected for.

3. Always praise (and offer a treat) as soon as he does something good (or when he stops doing something naughty). How else will he know he's a good dog?

4. Be consistent. You can't share the couch and watch television on Monday, then scold him for climbing onto the couch with you on Tuesday.

5. Never call your dog to you and correct him for something he did wrong. He will think the correction is for coming to you (think like a dog, remember?). Always go to the dog to stop unwanted behavior, but be sure you catch him in the act, or your dog will not understand the correction.

6. Never hit your dog or punish him physically in any way. Such physical measures will only create fear and confusion in your dog and could provoke aggressive behavior down the road.

7. When praising or correcting, use a light and happy voice. Conversely, use a firm, sharp voice for warnings or corrections. A whiny "no, no" or "drop that" will not sound convincing, nor will a deep, gruff voice when you say "good boy" make your puppy think he is doing something right.

BODY LANGUAGE

There is a definite language barrier between you and your Golden Retriever. However much you wish it were so, your Golden does not speak English. Dogs communicate through body language. It's up to you to learn what your dog's many postures mean and how to respond to them.

When your dog meets another animal—whether dog, cat, or human—he will convey his emotional response through his body posture. If you are familiar with these postures, you will better understand your Golden's behavior and mood and be able to predict your dog's next actions. Here are some common canine body postures that you may see in your Golden:

Neutral relaxed: While your Golden Retriever is just relaxing and enjoying life, he is in the neutral relaxed position with his head erect, ears up, and tail wagging. His mouth is partly open (with tongue possibly lolling), and his weight is evenly distributed over all four feet.

Greeting: When two dogs meet, they approach each other cautiously at first. The more dominant dog stands tall, holding his ears and tail high, while the more submissive dog hunches slightly, with ears back, tail down, and eyes semi-closed. The two sniff each other, learning the other's unique scent. It's a dog's way of saying hello!

Play bow: You see this stance a lot with Golden Retrievers. When your Golden wants to play, he lowers his front legs, pulling his head and shoulders toward the ground. His hind end is raised into the air with tail wagging happily.

Arousal: When your Golden is stimulated by something—whether it is a sight, smell, sound, or just a new experience—he strikes an arousal posture.

Make Your Puppy a S.T.A.R.

The American Kennel Club has a great program for new puppy owners called the S.T.A.R. Puppy® Program, which is dedicated to rewarding puppies that get off to a good start by completing a basic training class. S.T.A.R. stands for: Socialization, Training, Activity, and Responsibility.

You must enroll in a six-week puppy-training course with an AKC-approved evaluator. When the class is finished, the evaluator will test your puppy on all the training taught during the course, such as being free of aggression toward people and other puppies in the class, tolerating a collar or body harness, allowing his owner to take away a treat or toy, and sitting and coming on command.

If your puppy passes the test, he will receive a certificate and a medal. You and your puppy will also be listed in the AKC S.T.A.R. Puppy records. To learn more about the AKC S.T.A.R. Puppy Program or to find an approved evaluator near you, check out www.akc.org/starpuppy.

Rules for Training Puppies

1. Keep your pockets loaded with puppy treats at all times so you are prepared to reinforce good behavior whenever it occurs.

2. You are the "alpha dog" and your puppy's new pack leader. Be firm but fair, and if you don't know what you're doing, act like you do so your dog believes you.

3. Teach your Golden Retriever in a manner that he will understand. Don't expect him to understand every word you say.

4. Be nice. Goldens are sensitive dogs and do not like to be scolded or corrected. You will never gain your dog's trust if you're impatient, loud, or inconsistent.

When a strange new experience happens, your Golden lifts his head with ears held up and forward and shifts his weight forward over his front feet. His muzzle is tense, and his hackles may be up if it is something unfamiliar. If the experience is familiar, like a visitor to the front door, your Golden's muzzle relaxes, and his tail wags excitedly.

Defensive aggression: Golden Retrievers, being the friendly dogs that they are, rarely show an aggressive attack stance. However, it is good to know the pose so that you will recognize it if your dog or another dog were to approach you in this manner. If a dog feels threatened, he shows a defensive posture to warn the other dog (or animal) to stay away from him. His hackles are up, his tail is down, and his ears are back. His weight is shifted toward his back legs, and he may snarl and flash his teeth. If you come across a dog in this stance, do not approach him! The dog may very well lunge forward and bite you or your dog.

Submission: A submissive stance is the opposite of aggression. A submissive dog is surrendering himself to another animal, whether dog or human. There are two types of submissive postures that a dog may take: active and passive submission. Active submission is when a dog lowers his head and tail, lays his ears back, and half-closes his eyes. His mouth may be partially closed with his tongue darting in and out. Passive submission is when a dog rolls onto his back and exposes his belly to the dominant animal. He will tuck his tail and turn his head away, surrendering completely. Your Golden will strike this pose to let you know that you are his leader and show that he trusts you.

CLICKER TRAINING

Clicker training is a popular method of dog training that originated with dolphin trainers. Trainers use a small hand-held devise that emits a clicking sound when pressed. The clicker is pressed whenever the dog does something good (this is called "marking" the behavior), and a treat is immediately given. For example, when you cue your Golden to sit, click as soon as your dog's behind touches the floor and quickly toss him a treat. After a few days of training, your Golden will begin to associate the clicking sound with a reward. In time, he learns that by repeating the marked behavior, such as sitting, he can prompt you to make the clicking sound and give him a treat. Clicker training is a very effective form of positive reinforcement—it encourages the dog to focus on the lesson you are trying to teach and helps him understand exactly what you want him to do.

Use an upbeat, light tone when training your puppy. Your tone of voice is the most effective way to communicate with your Golden.

Playtime is important learning time for your Golden Retriever. Start teaching basic manners right away, such as coming when called or playing gently with humans.

A Golden Vocabulary

How many words can a dog understand? Some behaviorists believe that dogs can master a vocabulary to rival that of a chimpanzee, a parrot, or even a bright toddler. Beyond the command cues, such as *sit*, *down*, *stay*, and *heel*, dogs naturally learn words of things they like, such as cheese, treat, ball, walk, and toy. Performance dogs can learn dozens of words that relate to their pursuits. For example, agility competitors understand words such as weave, tunnel, slow, wait, easy, turn, up, and so forth. Owners can teach their Golden Retrievers the names of their toys or other objects around the house and train their dog to retrieve those objects. Some remarkable dogs have been known to recognize up to 200 individual words. Dogs also understand the human tone of voice and can very easily respond to full sentences even if they only understand one key word. "Are you ready to go *outside*?" "I think it's getting close to *suppertime*." "Such a nice sunny day for a *walk* around the block!" For a dog, it's the italics that matter!

THE SECRET OF PLAYTIME

Even though your Golden Retriever pup is young, there are still some easy ways to create a basic foundation for future obedience training. Playtime is a great way to start training your puppy—without him even realizing it! Try these simple and fun games to teach your Golden his first lessons.

Come Here, Golden!

The most important lesson you will teach your Golden Retriever is to come when you call his name. To help your Golden learn to come to you, sit on the floor on one side of the room and ask a friend to sit across from you on the other side. Place your puppy in the center of the room. Call to your puppy, saying "come" and his name in an upbeat and excited voice, patting the ground with your hands or clapping. Your Golden should run toward you happily. Once he reaches you, praise him and give him lots of pets and rubs. Now, have your friend call to your puppy, saying his name just as you did. Let the puppy run back and forth across the room each time he is called. Once he gets the idea, try extending the distance or moving outside in a secured, fenced area.

Your energetic Golden Retriever will need a strong foundation in basic obedience training. Start out with easy commands such as *come* and *sit* that you will use throughout your Golden's life.

Hide-and-Seek

A quick game of hide-and-seek will also teach your puppy to come when called. You can play this game inside the house or in the backyard, just be sure that the area is safely fenced before you begin. When your puppy is distracted, quickly hide behind a piece of furniture or around a corner. Keep it simple at first so that your puppy can find you easily. Using his name, say to your puppy, "Golden, where am I?" Your puppy should come running. When he finds you, congratulate and praise him. Keep repeating this game, making it a little more difficult each time. Soon, your Golden Retriever will be sniffing you out wherever you go.

Roughhouse

Get down on the carpet and wrestle gently with your puppy. If he gets overexcited and nips at your hands or arms, say "Ouch!" and sit back patiently. Wait until your Golden calms down, and only then begin playing again. This type of rough-housing play will teach your puppy what is and is not acceptable when playing with humans. Plus, it will help you both communicate through body language.

PUPPY KINDERGARTEN

A puppy socialization class or AKC S.T.A.R. Puppy class is a great way to introduce your puppy to basic training. Often called "puppy kindergarten," a puppy socialization class will allow your Golden to interact with other puppies his age. He will learn pack behavior—that is, how to play and communicate politely with other dogs. The trainer leading the class will watch your puppy to see if he acts unusual in any way, either overly shy or aggressive toward other dogs and people. Your puppy will also be introduced to walking on a leash as well as a few other simple exercises. Puppy kindergarten is a perfect first step in socializing your pup, with the added benefit of meeting new people and gaining the advice of a trained professional.

To find a puppy kindergarten class near you, ask your vet, breeder, local pet store, or dog-owning friends for referrals. Visit a class or two before signing up so that you can pick out the best environment and trainer for your Golden Retriever.

THE NEXT STEPS

After you begin basic training with your Golden Retriever, think ahead and try to decide which activities you feel you and your puppy would excel in. Whether you want to get involved in conformation, obedience, therapy, agility, or search and rescue, each activity will require a different set of training tools. Contact the American Kennel Club (www.akc.org), Golden Retriever Club of America (www.grca.org), or your local breed club for more information on all

Sign up for a puppy kindergarten class as soon as your Golden is old enough. He will learn basic manners, how to behave around other people and their dogs, and have a great time in the process!

of these activities and opportunities. These organizations can help you decide what methods of training to pursue next. Whatever you decide, remember that basic obedience training is a requirement for all dogs. Ongoing training throughout your dog's life will stimulate your Golden both mentally and physically and strengthen the bond between you and your dog for a lifetime.

At a Glance ...

Positive training is the most effective form of dog training. By rewarding good behavior and ignoring the not-so-good conduct, your puppy will soon learn what is expected of him.

• •

Training is not a simple one-day-a-week task. You must train your Golden Retriever constantly, with a consistent, patient, and determined attitude. Good training doesn't stop with house-training and leash-training. Continue to train your Golden throughout his life to build a trusting and lasting bond with your dog.

• •

Dogs don't speak English, but they do communicate through body language. Get to know your Golden's body language so that you can understand how he is adjusting to the world around him.

• •

Enroll your puppy in a puppy kindergarten class as soon as he receives all of his required immunizations. A puppy socialization class is a great way to introduce your puppy to other dogs and people, and it will create a basic training foundation for your Golden Retriever.

CHAPTER SIX

House-Training Etiquette

One of the most important lessons you will teach your Golden Retriever is when and where to go to the bathroom. House-training starts as soon as you bring your new puppy home—before you do anything, take your Golden to his potty spot. After the drive home from the breeder, chances are that he'll need to go, and when he does, praise him. Don't get angry if he doesn't grasp the idea of house-training right away. Remember that you are

teaching your Golden something completely unnatural for a dog—that there is a specific time and place to relieve himself. Expect to spend the next few weeks—or even months—helping your Golden Retriever understand the basics of house-training. With diligence, consistency, and patience, your puppy will be potty-trained in no time!

CRATE-TRAINING

Using a crate is the most reliable method of house-training a dog. A crate is perhaps the most important piece of dog equipment you will buy because it is actually a multi-purpose dog accessory. The crate is your Golden's personal dog house within your house; an effective and humane house-training tool; a security measure that will protect your puppy, home, and belongings when you're not home; a transportation vessel to house and protect your dog when you are traveling (most motels will accept a crated dog); and, finally, a comfy, confined space for your puppy when you need him not to be underfoot.

Because all canines are natural den creatures, thanks to the thousands of years their ancestors spent living in caves and burrows in the ground, your puppy will adapt quite naturally to his crate. Your Golden Retriever is inherently clean, and he will try hard not to soil his personal living space.

Many experienced breeders introduce their puppies to crates before they send them to their new homes and strongly encourage new owners to continue using the crate. If you're lucky enough to have found such a breeder, most of the house-training trials are already over! However, if your pup has never seen a crate, it's up to you to make his introduction to one a pleasant one.

Introduce the crate as soon as your Golden Retriever comes home so he learns that it is his new "house." This is best accomplished with dog treats. For the first day or two, toss a tiny treat into the crate to entice him to go in. Pick a crate cue, such as "kennel," "inside," or "crate," and use it every time he enters. You also can feed his meals inside the crate with the door open, so his associations with the crate will be happy ones.

As tempting as it will be to snuggle with your puppy in bed at night, don't do it! The alpha dog (you) should sleep on higher ground (in your bed) and the puppy should sleep in his crate. You don't want the puppy to think he's your equal; you want him to know you're his leader. At first, he may not like the accommodations, but he'll eventually quiet down and sleep. Again, don't be tempted to release him because he's fussing in his crate. If you open that crate door, you provide his first life lesson—if I cry, I get out and maybe even get a late-night snack and a hug. Here is a better plan: place the crate next to your bed at night for the first few weeks, turn off the lights, and go to sleep. Your presence will comfort him, and you'll also know if he needs a midnight potty trip.

Make a habit of placing your puppy in his crate for naps, at night-time, and whenever you are unable to watch him closely. Not to worry, he will let you know when he wakes up and needs to go out. If he falls asleep under the table and wakes up when you're not there, guess what he'll do first? Always keep a close eye on the puppy, and keep paper towels and cleaning supplies in every room!

Know when your puppy is most likely to "go"—right after a nap, a few minutes after meal times, after play periods, and whenever he's released from the crate (whether he was sleeping or not). A good rule of thumb is that most puppies under twelve weeks of age will need to eliminate once an hour, which is about a dozen times a day.

Always take your Golden Retriever outside to the same area, telling him "outside" as you go out. Pick a release cue, a word you're going to use to indicate that it's time to go potty. Common choices are "potty" or "get busy," but anything will work as long as you are consistent. After the pup's done his

A PIECE OF HISTORY

The first Golden Retriever to win an AKC Sporting Group and Best in Show title was Speedwell Pluto, a Golden imported from England in the 1930s as a personal gundog to Samuel S. Magoffin of North Vancouver, Canada. Pluto went on to establish the foundation breeding stock for the modern Golden Retriever in the American West.

business, be sure to praise him by saying "Good puppy!" and repeating your release cue. When taking the puppy outside, always use the same door and be sure the puppy can always get to that door to indicate he needs to go outside. The larger your house, the more vigilant you need to be.

CRATE ALTERNATIVES

If you've read this chapter and continue to shake your head and say, "I won't crate my baby," then here's a plan for you. It's not as effective as a crate, but it gives you a couple of options for what to do with your puppy when you're not home. Confine your Golden Retriever to one room with baby gates or other dog-proof barriers. Puppy-proof the room by removing anything the pup could hurt himself with or could chew or damage. Be forewarned, however; even in a stripped environment, pups will find something to chew (molding, door frames, paneling, drywall, floor tiles, and so forth).

Another alternative is to put up an exercise pen that measures 4-by-4 feet square (available through pet suppliers) that is sturdy enough so the pup can't knock it down. This X-pen provides safe containment for short periods. Paper one area for elimination and put a blanket in the opposite corner for napping. Safe chew toys should help keep your Golden content while you're gone.

PAPER-TRAINING

Paper-training is often used during the beginning stages of house-training, especially if you will be gone for long periods of the day and won't be able to take your

Stay consistent with your house-training methods. If you paper-train your Golden as a puppy, it may be difficult to train him to go outside later in life. Choose one method and stick with it.

Golden Retriever outside to his bathroom spot. However, keep in mind that it is difficult to train your puppy to go outside once he is paper-trained indoors. It's best to pick one method of house-training and stick to it so as not to confuse your puppy and delay your training progress.

If you feel that paper-training is the best option for your Golden, start by confining your puppy to a small room or a small area with an exercise pen. Cover the entire floor of the area with newspapers or pee pads. Place your Golden's crate, food, and water on one side of the area and give your puppy some toys to keep him occupied. Whenever you need to leave your puppy unsupervised, put him in this area. After a few days, you'll realize that your puppy will start going to the bathroom in one general area. One at a time, remove the papers from around the edges of your puppy's chosen potty spot. If he has an accident and goes on the floor, be patient and simply add some paper to the floor again. Eventually, your puppy will consistently relieve himself on one section of paper.

Slowly move this section of paper to the area in the house that you want your puppy to relieve himself, whether it is in a back laundry room or next to an outside door. But, whatever you do, go slowly so that your puppy understands what you

Part of house-training is being able to read your puppy's potty cues before he has an accident. All dogs have different ways of telling you they need to go. Some bark or run to the door, while others more subtly twitch or stare off into space.

If you want the signal to be a bit more obvious, try teaching your Golden Retriever to ring a bell when he wants to go outside. To teach this trick, hang a bell on the doorknob or on the wall next to the door that you always use to go to your dog's potty area. Make sure the bell is within your puppy's reach. Every time you take him on a potty run, ring the bell before you walk out the door. Eventually, your puppy will make the connection and start ringing the bell on his own. When he does, praise him and take him outside. The positive reinforcement will stick, and soon your Golden's potty cues will be clear as a bell.

want him to do. Soon, your Golden will be successfully paper-trained and know that the paper (or pad) is where he is expected to go.

THE GOLDEN RULES OF HOUSE-TRAINING

Rule #1: Never correct a puppy for relieving himself. No matter how carefully you watch your puppy, his bladder is only so big and you're only human. He will have accidents, and all you can do is act fast. If you catch him in a squat, clap your hands and make a loud noise to startle him and possibly interrupt him. Be sure to praise your Golden when he finishes his duty outside.

Rule #2: If you don't catch your Golden in the act, you have four seconds to do anything other than clean up. After that, your puppy will have no idea what you're talking about. Canines live in the moment and will not understand why you're clapping and screaming. Remember, peeing is as normal to a puppy as it

is to you. Hopefully your mother didn't scold you for going in your Pampers! If you discover the puddle five or ten seconds later, clean it up and watch more carefully next time for your puppy's warning signals, such as circling, sniffing, or whining.

Rule #3: Do not confine a young puppy in his crate for more than two hours unless he's sleeping. Here's the math: confine the puppy for a maximum of one hour for each month of his age; thus, three hours for a three-month-old pup, four to five hours for the four- to five-month-old, and six hours for dogs six months and older. Six hours is the max for any dog, regardless of age (except when he's sleeping at night)!

Rule #4: Never use the crate for punishment. Successful crate-training depends on your puppy's positive association with the crate. If your Golden associates the crate with "bad dog," he won't think of it as his safe place. Sure, you can crate your pup after he has sorted through the trash so you can clean up without being disturbed. Just don't do it in an angry fashion, but rather in a matter-of-fact, swift way before the puppy can process what you're thinking.

TIME AND PATIENCE

With patience and diligence, your Golden Retriever will become house-trained within a few weeks. The key is to stick to a scheduled routine of potty breaks and lots of praise. Expecting a dog to instinctively know to relieve himself outdoors isn't reasonable. You are trying to manipulate the animal's behavior so that he abides by our human rules. Don't get discouraged; it is possible. Millions of dogs are perfectly house-trained. Before you lose your temper with your puppy, take a deep breath and remember that training takes time. All your Golden Retriever wants to do is to please you. With dedication and determination, your puppy will be house-trained before you know it.

Don't let your puppy get distracted when you take him outside to do his business. After he goes, you can let your Golden explore the backyard.

At a Glance ...

Before you bring your Golden home, decide where you want your puppy to go to the bathroom and how you are going to house-train him. Whether you decide on paper-training or crate-training, stay consistent with your puppy, as not to confuse him and slow down your training process.

Crate-training is a proven and effective way of house-training your puppy. One of the common misconceptions of crate-training is that dogs dislike their crate. This is entirely untrue! Your Golden will learn to see his crate as his own safe haven where he can relax and sleep. You will continue to use his crate long after he is fully house-trained.

No matter how diligent you are, your Golden will have accidents in the house. When it happens, don't get angry at your Golden—you don't want him to think that relieving himself is wrong. Simply clean up the mess, and vow to catch him in the act the next time.

CHAPTER SEVEN

Top of the Class

Golden Retrievers are among the smartest of canines, sharing the honors with Border Collies, Poodles, and Labrador Retrievers. Goldens excel in virtually every canine pursuit and can be astonishingly quick at learning new tasks. Their intelligence combined with their desire to please their masters makes the Golden Retriever sensitive to correction. It takes patience to find the right blend of discipline, guidance, and praise in training your

Golden to be an obedient and well-mannered canine companion.

While we can't underestimate the importance of good manners at home, obedience in the community goes a lot further. For your Golden to be welcome wherever you go, he must learn basic obedience cues. More importantly, for his own safety, your dog should be proficient in simple cues such as *come, sit, stay, down*, and *heel*.

READY, SET, TRAIN

Start your puppy's lessons as soon as he comes home. There's a lot to learn, and it's never too early to start. His prime learning period is the first twenty weeks of his life, so the process is easier and will be more successful if you start right away. Choose a quiet place, free from distractions, to begin your pup's education. Once your Golden Retriever has learned a cue, change the setting and practice in a different location—another room, the yard, then with another person or with a dog nearby. If your puppy reacts to the new distraction and does not perform the exercise, back up and remove the distractions for a while. Don't rush things. Remember that he's just a puppy!

Don't go straight from playtime to school time. You want your Golden to be focused on training. It's better to put your puppy in his crate for some quiet time before you begin a lesson. He will be delighted to spend time with you when you release him from his crate, and he will be eager to pay attention to you.

Brevity is key for training puppies. A four- or five-minute lesson is all a ten-week-old puppy can handle. After a couple of weeks, your Golden should be ready for a longer session. Vary the lessons so that your dog doesn't know what to expect next. By altering the exercises, you're keeping your canine student interested and the lesson fun. As soon as you see your dog losing focus, end the lesson with a cue your dog has mastered and throw a ball to take a break.

Puppies love praise in the form of petting, sweet talk, and treats. A puppy that receives a pat and a tasty tidbit will always have fun and feel he's doing something productive. It's important for you to be happy, upbeat, and patient for all training sessions. If you can't be all three on the same day, it's not a school day. Golden Retrievers are sensitive and will think that your impatient mood is

Once your Golden can perform basic cues with ease, add a few distractions. Take your Golden outside and run through his lessons with another person or dog nearby.

a reflection on them. Don't take a step backward by quitting a lesson on a failed cue. If the puppy isn't picking up a new exercise, repeat a lesson he knows well so that the session will end on a positive note with a big "good boy!" and a happy rub on his neck.

THAT'S MY NAME!

If your puppy hasn't mastered this already, you can begin with this lesson to teach him to respond to his name. Start by calling your Golden Retriever's name when he is paying attention. When he responds and looks at you, toss him a tasty treat. Practice throughout the first day, and he will learn two things immediately. First, he will recognize his name, and second, that you're definitely the right person to follow because you're always flinging food his way. Food makes everything positive, including his name.

TWO CUES TO START

Let's begin by teaching two cues that will be useful throughout your Golden's life. The first cue, *take it*, is essentially granting the puppy permission; the second, *leave it*, is a positive way of saying no. You can teach the *take it* cue by using a treat. Hold a treat in your hand, raise your hand to the pup's muzzle, and say "take it." There's nothing to it! Hand. Food. Take it. Done.

Do this a few times, saying "take it." At this point, the puppy really doesn't think "take it" has any more meaning than "yummy," so you have to underscore its meaning. Next time the pup goes to take the treat from your hand, close your hand and hold it closed. He'll sniff and nuzzle, but do nothing except hold your hand steady. When he gives up, count to five, and then open your palm and say "take it." From this point on, you can extend the amount of time you keep your hand closed on the treat before allowing your dog to "take it."

Be the Teacher

You have established yourself as your puppy's alpha so you should be his primary teacher. During the early stages of his education, having only one person lead the lessons will help to avoid confusion for your puppy. Once your Golden has learned a command reliably, have another family member participate and practice the command with the pup. Be sure everyone who works with the puppy uses the same cues and knows how to treat him during the lesson.

The second cue is an extension or variation on this exercise. Hold out your palm with the treat to the dog and say "leave it." Immediately close your hand as the pup tries to nab the treat and repeat the cue. Repeat this again and again until he pulls away and waits. Now you can say "take it" and let him have the treat. Gradually increase the time before you allow the pup to have the treat.

Now let's apply this lesson to real life. Retrievers love to pick things up and carry them around. Puppies tend to pick up the smelliest stuff possible, like used cellophane from the trash can, socks and underwear from the hamper, diapers from the pail, and worse.

Stand in front of your puppy (who should be on a loose lead) and toss a squeaky toy behind you. As the puppy looks toward it, say "leave it." Block him with your body if he attempts to go for the toy. Continue for as long as it takes for him to lose interest, and then say "take it" and get out of the way. Do this a few times, using different toys or treats, so he understands that he must wait for your cue to retrieve the toy.

COME

Fortunately, Golden Retrievers like being close to their people, so teaching the *come* cue is not difficult. The key to this exercise is to brainwash your puppy into believing that all good stuff comes from you. When your puppy hears you say, "come, Golden," he will instantly want to see what you're doing or, better yet, what treats you are going to give him.

This exercise is arguably the most important lesson you will teach your dog. An obedient dog that comes when called is less likely to run into danger, step into oncoming traffic, or dash after a squirrel. It's best to practice this exercise with the puppy on his leash and in the familiar, safe surroundings of your fenced-in yard.

Can Your Dog Pass the Canine Good Citizen® Test?

An AMERICAN KENNEL CLUB Program

Once your Golden Retriever is ready for advanced training, you can start training him for the American Kennel Club Canine Good Citizen® Program. This program is for dogs that are trained to behave at home, out in the neighborhood, and in the city. It's easy and fun to do. Once your dog learns basic obedience and good canine manners, a CGC evaluator gives your dog ten basic tests. If he passes, he's awarded a Canine Good Citizen® certificate. Many trainers offer classes with the test as the final to graduate from the class. To find an evaluator in your area, go to www.akc .org/events/cgc/cgc_bystate.cfm.

Many therapy dogs and guide dogs are required to pass the Canine Good Citizen® test in order to help as working dogs in the community. There are ten specific skills that a dog must master in order to pass the Canine Good Citizen® test. A well-trained dog will:

1. Let a friendly stranger approach and talk to his owner.
2. Let a friendly stranger pet him.
3. Be comfortable being groomed and examined by a friendly stranger.
4. Walk on a leash and show that he is in control and not overly excited.
5. Move through a crowd politely and confidently.
6. Sit and stay on command.
7. Come when called.
8. Behave calmly around another dog.
9. Not bark at or react to a surprise distraction.
10. Show that he can be left with a trusted person away from his owner.

In order to help your dog pass the AKC CGC test, first enroll him in basic training classes or a CGC training class. You can find classes and trainers near you by searching the AKC website. When you feel that your Golden is ready to take the test, locate an AKC-approved CGC evaluator to set up a test date, or sign up for a test that is held at a local AKC dog show or training class. For more information about the AKC Canine Good Citizen® Program, visit www.akc.org/events.cgc.

Tone of voice is very important when training your dog, and this is one instance in which a happy, carefree tone works best. Stand a few yards from your puppy, and while he's watching, say "come, Golden," clap your hands, and show him a treat. In true Golden Retriever style, your puppy should come barreling toward you. When he gets to you, give him the treat and say "good boy." On the off-chance that he's distracted and hesitates to come to you, give his leash a friendly tug and he'll come toward you. Hold his collar with one hand while you give him a treat. Later, you'll practice this exercise without treats and simply reward him with a pat on the head.

Practice the *come* cue as often as you possibly can during the puppy's first few days at home. Your goal is to train your puppy to come to you every time you call without hesitation. Don't chintz on the treats or praise—reward your Golden Retriever every time he comes to you. When practicing outside, be sure to keep a leash on the dog. Some Goldens go instantly deaf when they see a pigeon rustling in the leaves or a chipmunk scampering over the pavement. No pat or liver treat is more enticing than a twittering chipmunk!

Stopping Separation Anxiety

A dog with separation anxiety exhibits extreme behavior problems when left alone. After his owner leaves the house, the dog has a panic response and will dig, chew, or scratch at the door trying to get to his owner. He will howl, cry, and bark, and may even urinate or defecate from distress.

Some things seem to trigger separation anxiety. Dogs that are used to constantly being with their owners but are suddenly left alone for the first time may exhibit panicky behavior. A traumatic event, such as time spent in a shelter or kennel, may also trigger anxiety. A change in the family's routine or structure, such as a child leaving for college, can also cause stress in a dog's life.

If you believe your Golden is suffering from separation anxiety, here are some ways to address the problem:

● Keep your departures and arrivals low-key. Quietly leave the house and ignore your dog for a few minutes before acknowledging him when you return.

● Leave your dog with an item of clothing that smells like you.

● If your dog chews excessively when you are gone, leave him with a chew toy filled with treats.

More severe cases of separation anxiety require you to systematically train your dog to get used to being alone. Discuss options with your veterinarian and trainer—they may be able to offer more long-term solutions, such as prescription drugs for separation anxiety that can be used during behavior-modification training.

Talk to a Professional

If you are having trouble training your exuberant Golden Retriever, don't hesitate to ask for extra help. A professional dog trainer can be a big help, getting you on the right track with your Golden and showing you how to deal with his problem behaviors. When looking for a trainer, ask your veterinarian or breeder, and search the websites of organizations such as the Association of Pet Dog Trainers (www.apdt.com) or the Certification Council for Professional Dog Trainers (www.ccpdt.org). You can also contact the GRCA (www.grca.org) for advice on where to find the right trainer for you and your Golden.

SIT

The food-happy Golden Retriever can be taught to sit in no time. Teaching *sit* requires little more than standing in front of the dog and holding a tasty morsel over his nose. As you move the treat over his head, he will sit so that he's in a better position to chomp. Now say "sit" in a convincing voice. *Voila!* You've have taught your puppy to sit!

Sometimes your puppy will lift himself back up to reach the treat, in which case you simply lower it. Once the puppy holds the *sit* for a moment, give him the treat. It's important that your dog make the mental association between the exercise, the cue, and the food reward.

After you've practiced this a dozen times or so, have your Golden remain in the sit position for longer periods before you release the treat. The dog's patience in waiting for the treat is actually the foundation for our next exercise, the *stay*. You don't have to plan formal lesson time to review the *sit* or any other cue. It's better to incorporate the exercises into everyday life. For example, have your puppy sit before you give him his dinner, before a guest greets him, and before you present him with a new toy or bone.

Teach your dog to stay by first instructing him to sit. Keep him in the sit position for a few seconds and then release him.

STAY

The easiest part about the *stay* cue is that there's really nothing for the dog to do. The hardest part is that there's really nothing for the dog to do. A Golden Retriever puppy is always aching to do, do, do and please his human, so a few seconds of "staying" can be real work. This cue can be taught as part two of the sit exercise. The puppy, in his seated position, is signaled by your palm and cued to "stay." While you count to five, the puppy does nothing except wait for something to happen. That something is your release words, "OK, good boy." Give your puppy elaborate praise, and practice the *sit* and *stay* cues again, stretching the times each time.

The next part of the lesson is to step backward once the puppy is in the sit/ stay position. Then extend the time and the number of steps. If the puppy tries to get up, tell him "no" and move closer. Don't get too ambitious and attempt to make your puppy sit for more than fifteen or twenty seconds. A stay that lasts longer than twenty seconds, in a young puppy's mind, is a nap.

DOWN

Depending on your dog and his personality, the *down* cue can be a challenging exercise to master. If your puppy is very outgoing and high-strung, it will take some patience to get him to assume a submissive posture. For more laid-back puppies, the *down* shouldn't be too tough as long as you have established a trusting bond with your puppy. Regardless of your Golden Retriever's temperament, it's best to begin teaching the *down* cue when the puppy is young.

Holding a treat over your puppy's head, cue your Golden to sit. Instead of giving him the treat upon sitting, move the treat from his nose toward his paws to the floor and then move it back along the ground, drawing it out, away from his front paws. He should move his front legs forward toward the treat and his belly to the floor. When he assumes this down position, give him the treat and praise him. After a week or so of practicing the *down*, add the *stay* cue.

HEEL

Without adequate leash training, an exuberant 70-pound adult Golden Retriever is no pleasure to walk! Walking your dog should be a mutually enjoyable, healthy activity, not one that you dread because your Golden isn't well behaved on his leash. There's no doubt that leash training needs to happen while your Golden is young, before he can drag you down the boulevard!

At the very least, your Golden should be trained to walk politely by your side, even if he never masters formal heel training like you see in the obedience ring. There are no special tricks to teaching a puppy to walk on a leash. It's a matter of communicating with your dog that you are the leader and he needs to follow your directions and commands.

From the day he arrives home, your puppy should wear a simple buckle collar. Every day for the first few weeks, attach a light nylon leash to the puppy's collar for five to ten minutes. Now all you have to do is supervise as your puppy drags the leash around the house or yard. If your puppy starts playing with the leash or chewing it, simply distract him with a toy or a game of fetch. Do not give him a treat to distract him or else he'll think you're rewarding him for chewing on his leash.

Attach the leash only when you have time to watch the puppy and play some games with him. He will soon gain a positive association with wearing the leash. After three or four days, you can take one end of the leash and walk around the yard or the living room. Be upbeat but nonchalant about these first few steps. The puppy should be on your left side, and you should talk to him and praise him while you're walking. Use a food lure to keep the

Walking your dog is fun if you train him to heel. A large dog like the Golden Retriever that is untrained will make every walk a tug-of-war!

puppy close to you. After a short distance (a yard or two), give him the treat and some belly rubs.

Once your puppy gets comfortable with the idea of walking on a leash, you can start teaching the basics of *heel*. Start with your Golden on your left side in the sit position. Hold the leash short in your left hand, with the excess leash in your right hand. Say "heel" and step forward with your left foot, keeping the dog close to your side as you step forward three paces. Stop and return him to the sit position. Each time he heels and sits correctly, praise him lavishly with your words, but don't touch him. Keep repeating this exercise until your Golden looks to you for the cue to heel and sit.

Practice this lesson a few times a day for a minute or two, but don't overdo it. Puppies have very short attention spans and they live only for fun and rewards. Once the puppy is walking with ease at your side, begin turning in one direction and then another. Introduce a verbal cue (like "walk" or "let's go"), and always give the puppy a treat after the exercise is completed.

PUPPY CLASSES

Practicing at home is just the beginning of training your Golden Retriever. Find a local breed club in your area by visiting the AKC website at www.akc.org or the GRCA website at www.grca.org. Local clubs offer puppy-training classes that all owners can take advantage of. You may also be able to find a training class through your veterinarian or pet-supply store.

Because Golden Retrievers are so intelligent, you must invest the time and effort to properly train your dog. If you need help training your Golden, seek out a professional dog trainer.

The American Kennel Club sponsors an incentive program called the S.T.A.R. Puppy® Program for all puppy owners who have completed a six-week training course instructed by an AKC-approved CGC evaluator. You can enroll your Golden in the S.T.A.R. Puppy Program and when he passes the final test, he'll receive a medal indicating that he's a S.T.A.R. Puppy. The acronym stands for Socialization, Training, Activity, and Responsibility. (See page 55, or visit http://www.akc.org/starpuppy/ for more information.)

Beyond the S.T.A.R. Puppy Program, your Golden can pursue the Canine Good Citizen title, a test that proves that your dog has mastered the ten basic skills of a well-mannered dog. The Canine Good Citizen® Program is so highly regarded that certain insurance companies offer a discount for dogs that have earned the title, and most therapy-dog registries require that the title is earned prior to certification. (See page 75, and learn more at http://www.akc.org/events/cgc/.)

A GOLDEN OPPORTUNITY

The Golden Retriever is an amazing breed that can be taught to do great things once he's learned basic good behavior. If you feel like your Golden Retriever has the potential to become an assistance, search and rescue, or therapy dog, stay on the path of good training. Get involved in your local breed club to learn about these opportunities and about further training. As with any animal serving the community, requirements include good behavior and impeccable training. As one of the most trainable AKC breeds, your Golden Retriever has the ability to achieve any training goal you set your mind to. All it takes is time, dedication, and a whole lot of treats.

At a Glance ...

Basic obedience training is a must for your exuberant Golden Retriever. Teaching your dog to *come*, *sit*, *stay*, *heel*, and *take it* and *leave it* will reinforce your bond with your puppy as well as protect him from possibly dangerous situations.

The American Kennel Club's S.T.A.R. Puppy Program is a great way to get your puppy on the right training track. Once your puppy has mastered basic obedience skills, begin training for the Canine Good Citizen test. This obedience exam tests the basic skills necessary for well-mannered dogs to coexist and interact successfully within the community.

Basic training provides a foundation for future, more advanced training with your Golden Retriever. Start researching the activities—such as conformation, field events, obedience, agility, therapy, or rally—that you may want to participate in with your Golden at the AKC website, www.akc.org, and the Golden Retriever Club of America website, www.grca.org, to determine the best course of training for your Golden.

CHAPTER EIGHT

Food Fit for a Golden

Nothing will entice your Golden Retriever more than food. The sound of clattering stainless steel, the crinkling of a paper sack, the unmistakable aroma of fresh meat in the air—all will bring your Golden running. Your Golden Retriever should have the best food you can afford. Only a premium-quality food will provide the proper balance of vitamins, minerals, and fatty acids necessary to develop healthy bones, muscles, skin, and coat on a

Changing Diets

When you bring your Golden home, be careful about changing to a completely different dog food right away. That quick change could make your dog sick. If you plan to switch from the food fed by his breeder, take home a small supply of the breeder's food to mix with your own. Make the change slowly to aid in your puppy's adjustment to his new food.

growing dog. The major dog-food manufacturers have developed age-appropriate formulas with strict quality controls, using only the best ingredients. It's unnecessary to add supplements or extra vitamins unless you've been instructed to do so by a veterinarian or your breeder.

YOU ARE WHAT YOU EAT

In the United States, the nutritional standards of store-bought dog foods are tested by the Association of American Feed Control Officials (AAFCO). In order for a company to claim its dog food is "complete and balanced," the food must contain a variety of ingredients following the nutritional standards set by the

AAFCO. Labels on dog-food packaging list ingredients in descending order of weight or amount. Do your research to find the right dog food for your Golden based on his weight, age, and activity level. Here are a few types of nutrients you will find on most dog-food labels:

- **Carbohydrates:** Carbohydrates act as the main energy source for your Golden. They are broken down and converted into sugars in your dog's body.
- **Fats:** When carbohydrates can't do the job alone, fats are stored and broken down as a secondary energy source. They also help in the production of hormones and in nervous-system function.
- **Proteins:** Proteins help restore and repair muscle, bone, and other body tissues. They also play a major role in immune-system function. Beware of too much protein, however, as it can cause itchy, dry skin or even kidney problems.
- **Vitamins:** Vitamins help stimulate growth, healing, and muscular and nervous function in your Golden.
- **Water:** Daily water intake washes away excess waste in your dog's body. Be sure to have ample, clean water available to your Golden at all times.

LIFESTAGE FORMULAS

Premium dog-food brands now offer foods for various sizes, ages, and activity levels. Puppies require a diet different than adults, as do seniors. Choose the best formula for your Golden Retriever based on his age, weight, and lifestyle. Whatever you choose, keep your dog lean to help prevent hip dysplasia.

Puppy Formulas

When your puppy was first weaned from his mother, your breeder most likely introduced small amounts of canned meat to tempt him from his mother's milk. Once he reached eight weeks, the breeder then began to feed him a puppy food specially formulated for growth that contained protein and fat levels appropriate for a growing Golden. Large-breed, fast-growing dogs like the Golden require more protein and fat during these early months of development.

While your puppy is growing, seek out a growth-formula puppy food specially made for large-breed dogs. He will need to eat four meals throughout the day to stimulate his growth and keep his metabolism charged and functioning. As your puppy grows through his adolescence, transition to a two-meals-a-day routine, but stick with the growth formula until he is at least one year old.

A PIECE OF HISTORY

The first dog treat was created in the mid-1800s by an American electrician named James Spratt, who observed stray dogs at the shipyard eating sailors' discarded biscuits. He began to make a biscuit specially crafted for dogs, made of wheat meal, vegetables, and meat. By the turn of the century, his "meat-fibrine dog cakes" were popular throughout the United States and England.

Buy the best dog food you can afford. Premium diets are made with high-quality ingredients and will result in healthy dogs with shiny coats.

Adult and Senior Formulas

Once your Golden is fully grown, around twelve to eighteen months, he'll require an adult-food formula that is based on weight maintenance. At this age, your Golden should only be fed twice a day, and the type of food and amount should be based on your dog's age, current weight, and activity level. Beware of feeding your dog too much at once. Large dogs may gobble their food, resulting in gastric torsion, or bloat, a life-threatening condition in which trapped air and food causes a dog's stomach to twist, cutting off blood flow and damaging internal organs in the process. Prevent bloat by monitoring your dog's eating habits and, if necessary, by choosing food bowls designed to slow down your dog as he eats.

These types of bowls have folds, crevices, and pacer balls that force your dog to navigate around the obstacles and therefore take smaller, slower bites.

As your dog transitions into his senior years, around seven years old, his metabolism begins to slow down. He is less active and sleeps more; don't be surprised if he gains weight on his current adult diet. If you notice that your senior Golden is starting to get pudgy, switch to a senior formula, which contains more nutrients needed for your aging dog and less calories to prevent weight gain and obesity. Consult with your veterinarian whenever you change your dog's feeding habits. Your vet will help you decide what's best for your Golden Retriever based on his weight, age, and activity level.

SO MANY CHOICES

When you walk the dog-food aisles in your local pet-supply store, you will be overwhelmed by the selection available—in cans, bags, and frozen packages. Even experienced dog people can get lost in the ever-growing world of doggy nutrition. Don't let the vast variety intimidate you! Begin by reading the food labels to find out what's inside. If you're intrigued by a certain brand or variety, call the manufacturer's information number. Ask your breeder and your vet what food they recommend for your Golden Retriever puppy. If you plan to switch from the food fed by your breeder, take home a small supply of the breeder's food to mix with your own to help your puppy's adjustment to his new food.

Should you feed canned or dry food? Should you offer dry food with or without water? Is it okay to add fresh chicken or hamburger to jazz up the dry food? There are so many questions that you probably have concerning your dog's food. The first choice you need to make is what type of food to feed your dog. Dry, semi-moist, and canned are the three most popular food choices, and each have pros and cons depending on your Golden's tastes and lifestyle.

Kibble: Dry food is recommended by most veterinarians because the dry particles help clean teeth of plaque and tartar. It is also the most economical

Prevent Poor Eating Habits

The easiest way to prevent poor eating habits is not to encourage the behavior from the start. Your Golden Retriever will soon learn to eat his meals in a certain place at scheduled times, rather than expecting to join your dinner hour. He will also be far less likely to pick at his food or dawdle over his dinner if he knows it's going to be served and taken away at specific times. Uneaten food should be picked up after twenty minutes. Scheduled feeding not only discourages picky eating habits, it also helps prevent obesity.

option and is easily digestible for your young Golden. Adding water to dry food is a good idea, especially if your dog inhales his food or is a picky eater. A splash of warm water added immediately before eating will enhance the flavor of the food. If you'd like to add a little fresh meat to your dog's food, he won't complain. Just don't overdo it by adding too much or making it a fixture of his mealtime. He'll get fussy when you run out of hamburger and offer him just plain kibble.

Semi-moist: If your Golden turns his nose up at dry food, semi-moist may be a good food to try. It is soft to the bite, and it is shaped and colored to look like treats for all of those finicky eaters out there. Because of its soft texture, it's also a good choice for senior Goldens with sensitive teeth and gums. Check the ingredient label on the packaging before buying, as many semi-moist foods contain high amounts of corn syrup and preservatives to make the food taste better. These ingredients can cause weight gain in your Golden Retriever and will negatively affect his dental health.

Canned: Canned food is the most expensive option, but most dogs consider it the tastiest. Choice cuts of meat and vegetables are prepackaged with gravy in cans. At 70 percent water, this type of food will keep your Golden more hydrated than dry or semi-moist foods. Canned food has a long shelf life, so it is easy to buy in bulk, however, once you open a can, it must be refrigerated immediately and used within a few days. Also, if your Golden has any digestive problems, the high water content may cause diarrhea as well as plaque and tartar buildup on teeth.

THE GOURMET ALTERNATIVE

If you've scoured the aisles of the pet-supply store and you can't find a food with the nutrition you feel your dog needs to thrive, there are a few alternatives to commercial dog foods. Both fresh and home-cooked diets allow owners to know exactly what they are feeding their dogs and be assured that all the ingredients are fresh and of human-grade quality.

Your Golden puppy needs a diet high in protein and fat to support his growing body and unflagging energy. Discuss the right food choice with your veterinarian.

Go Natural!

Fresh dog foods can be found in the refrigerator section at pet-supply stores. These specialty "natural" foods feature high-quality protein sources, such as chicken, turkey, fish, and beef, prepared with minimal processing and no preservatives. Certain brands of natural foods have higher percentages of proteins and are free of grains, starches, and other fillers, boasting added antioxidants and Omega fatty acids. More easily digestible than other foods, fresh varieties are a godsend for picky eaters. The high protein content in natural dog food is suitable for large-breed puppies and active, working dogs. Some veterinarians recommend these natural foods for older or recuperating dogs as well as for pregnant dams and dogs with grain sensitivity or skin or digestive problems.

Home-Cooked Cuisine

If your dog is an especially picky eater or is allergic to a variety of common pet-food ingredients, a home-cooked diet may be the choice for you. Home-cooked diets are made from whole ingredients such as potatoes, rice, vegetables, chicken, and beef that are free from preservatives and artificial sweeteners. Your vet can point you to different resources to find the perfect balanced diet for your Golden Retriever. You will have to keep track of safe ingredients for your dog and maintain a healthy balance of vitamins and nutrients in his everyday diet. Golden

Retrievers also eat quite a lot, so be sure to use recipes that can be made in bulk and frozen between meals.

As always, be sure to consult a veterinarian or veterinary nutritionist before changing your Golden's diet. Switching to a home-cooked diet is a big change in both your life and your Golden's, so be sure to research all the details and options so that you can make an informed decision.

THE DINNER BELL

An eight-week-old puppy does best eating four times a day. At about twelve weeks of age, you can switch to three-times-daily feeding. Once the dog is twelve to eighteen months of age, most breeders suggest two meals a day for the life of the dog for better digestion and bloat prevention. Free-feeding, that is, leaving a bowl of dry food available all day, is not recommended for the ever-famished Golden. Not only can this lead to your dog becoming a picky eater, but a free-feeder is also more likely to become possessive of his food bowl.

Scheduled meals are also good training times; they give you an opportunity to remind your Golden that all good things in life come from you. Regular meals help you know how much your puppy eats and when, which is valuable information for weight control and recognizing changes in appetite. Another bonus of scheduled meals is your ability to predict your Golden's elimination, which simplifies house-training.

NO SECONDS, PLEASE

Like people, puppies and adult dogs have different appetites: some will lick their food bowls clean and beg for more, while others pick at their food and leave some of it untouched. Be careful not to overfeed the dog that is always hungry. Plump puppies may be cute and cuddly, but the extra weight will stress their growing joints. Overweight puppies tend to grow into overweight adults that tire easily and are more susceptible to health problems. Consult your breeder and your veterinarian for advice on how to adjust meal portions as your puppy grows.

It's always best to err on the side of "lean." Vets agree that lean dogs (like people) live longer, healthier lives and are less likely to develop hip dysplasia. The heavier the dog, the less likely he is to exercise and stay active. Golden Retrievers are happiest when they're running and jumping, so hold back on the extra treat or piece of cheese. Never feed your dog from the table; it only encourages begging, which is never welcome. Be careful when offering your dog people food. Safe people foods include cheese, apples, plain popcorn, bits of cooked chicken, and peanut butter. Dangerous foods include chocolate, onions, grapes, raisins and certain nuts—all of which are toxic to dogs.

The bottom line: What and how much you feed your Golden is a major factor in his overall health and longevity. It's worth your investment in time and money to provide the best diet for your dog.

At a Glance ...

Learn to read the nutrition labels on dog-food packaging. Though all commercial dog foods must follow the standards of the Association of American Feed Control Officials (AAFCO), only you know what ingredients and nutrients are needed for your Golden Retriever to thrive based on his age, size, and activity level.

Research the different dog-food options: dry, semi-moist, and canned. Each type has pros and cons depending on the tastes and needs of your individual Golden Retriever.

If you feel that a raw or home-cooked diet is the best choice for your Golden, discuss the details with your veterinarian or veterinary nutritionist before making the change. Alternative diets require ample research and planning to be successful and safe for your Golden Retriever.

Always have plenty of fresh water available for your Golden Retriever. Water is an important part of your dog's diet and is crucial for his overall health and well-being.

CHAPTER NINE

A Golden Beauty

Y ou can't really love a Golden Retriever without loving his golden fur! And Goldens have a lot of fur to love. To keep your dog's coat healthy and clean, you must designate regular grooming time. During the Golden's two shedding seasons—about three weeks in the spring and again in the fall—you will need to brush your dog at least once or twice a day. The rest of the year requires brushing every other day to keep your Golden's coat under

control. The more shed hair you can capture in a brush, the less hair you will have around your home. As lovely as golden fur looks on your dog, it's not so appealing on your furniture, clothing, or dinner plate.

Establish a grooming regimen while your Golden is a puppy. Brushing is as vital to his physical well-being as exercise and diet. Grooming should be a part of the dog's weekly routine all year long. Besides caring for the coat, skin, ears, teeth, and nails, grooming is a safety check for lumps, bumps, hot spots, and other abnormalities that can hide beneath your dog's thick coat. It will also uncover unwelcome parasites—fleas and ticks—that may have taken up residence on your dog.

Most Goldens are very in tune with their owner's feelings and moods. If your approach to grooming is "let's get this over with so I can go shopping," your dog will know it and feel uneasy. Don't rush through the process. Choose a quiet time of the day instead of the morning when you're rushed or just before dinner while you are cooking. Make your dog feel like this time is about him and not simply a quick chore you need to get out of the way. Your Golden Retriever will enjoy

During the warm summer months, bathe your Golden outside in a small tub or baby pool. Gather all your bathing supplies and make sure the water is warm enough.

the hands-on attention and the bonding that naturally accompanies the grooming process. Don't be afraid to incorporate petting and hugging and sweet talk in your grooming sessions. Even Goldens like to hear: "Who's the prettiest boy?"

Older dogs that aren't accustomed to regular grooming sessions may resist and be uncooperative. Fighting with a full-grown Golden will definitely make grooming feel like a distasteful chore, even a battle, rather than a routine procedure that both of you can and should enjoy.

HAIR, HAIR, EVERYWHERE!

Hold your first grooming session as soon as your Golden has adjusted to his new home and family. Start by letting the puppy smell the brush. Don't let him chew it or play with it, but let him sniff it and get familiar with it; this removes the mystery of the strange object before you start using it. Start by stroking your

dog gently with a soft brush, then handle his paws and ears, and gently touch his gums. Assure him with lots of happy sweet talk and a couple of treats at the end of the session. Keep it positive and fun—the only one who should know that grooming is a required chore is you.

The adult Golden has a medium-length double coat, with an undercoat that varies in density depending on the dog and the climate in which you live. Regular brushing removes dirt and debris and distributes the oils that keep your dog's coat clean and conditioned; more frequent brushing is needed during the breed's spring and fall shedding seasons.

The best time to brush your Golden is after his daily walk, as he will be more relaxed and his coat may have dirt or grass stuck in it from his time outside. Use a pin brush or a slicker brush with curved metal bristles. As you brush through your Golden's coat, be sure to look for signs of fleas, ticks, or skin problems. Pay attention to any tangled burrs or mats in the fur, and be gentle with your brush. Your Golden's skin is sensitive, and you don't want to scratch him by brushing too vigorously. As you brush, you'll notice a lot of hair gathering in the bristles. This is completely normal. Try to catch all the loose hair you can in your brush. After thoroughly brushing your pup, use a thin, stainless-steel comb to remove any hair your slicker brush may have missed.

Brush your Golden every other day, and every day during the shedding seasons. This will keep his golden coat silky and shiny. Your Golden will learn to love his grooming sessions because it's more time spent with you. Not only does he get praise and treats from you, but he also gets a full-body massage and rubdown. What more could a dog ask for?

Did You Know?

The American Veterinary Dental Society states that 80 percent of dogs show signs of oral disease as early as age three. Further studies prove that good oral hygiene can add three to five years to a dog's life. There's nothing like a twelve-year-old Golden flashing his pearly whites at his happy owner!

Lumps and Ticks and Patches, Oh My!

Your weekly grooming sessions should include body checks for lumps (cysts, warts, and fatty tumors), hot spots, and other skin or coat problems. While harmless skin lumps are common in older dogs, many can be malignant, and your veterinarian should examine any abnormality. Black mole-like patches or growths on any body part require immediate veterinary inspection. Be extra-conscious of dry skin, a flaky coat, and thinning hair, all signs of possible thyroid disease. Check for fleas and flea dirt (especially on your dog's underside and around the base of the tail) if you think fleas could be present.

A GOOD BATH

Frequent bathing is seldom necessary and, in fact, will remove the essential oils that keep your dog's skin supple and coat firm, gleaming and, most importantly, water-repellent. If you brush him regularly, your dog will only need a bath once every couple of months—more often if he plays in mud holes and rolls around in foul-smelling things (a favorite Golden pastime). In these cases, the dog simply needs a nice warm bath!

While it's a rare Golden that doesn't like water, bath time can be a challenge if your dog doesn't like being in the tub, the smell of soap, or the feeling of lather on his body. To minimize the stress and struggle of bathing, introduce your pup to bathing when he's young, and make bath time fun!

Lure your puppy into the tub with something extra tasty, like a cube of cheese or a spoonful of peanut butter. Line the tub or shower with a rubber mat for safe footing. Start by placing your puppy in the tub with no water. Once he's comfortable there, gradually add shallow water, then wet him down. Add one more step of the bathing process each time. Your Golden Retriever may never learn to love the bath, but all you need is cooperation. If it's summertime, you can bathe your dog in a small tub or baby pool in the backyard. Just be sure that the water is warm enough so your puppy doesn't get chilled.

Always brush your Golden thoroughly before getting his coat wet. Mats that form in the coat will only get larger and tighter when wet. Once your dog is brushed from head to toe, thoroughly wet him in the tub with warm (not hot) water. Use a shampoo made specially for dogs, as human shampoos and soaps will dry out your dog's skin. After shampooing, rinse the coat completely to avoid any itching from residual soap.

A chamois is the ideal tool for drying because it absorbs water like a sponge. If you need to, use a hair dryer on low heat, and hold it at least three feet from your dog as you dry his fur. Keep him away from drafts after bathing until he is completely dry to prevent chilling. Spritz-on dry shampoos are handy in case you need a quick cleanup to remove dirt and body odor.

NAIL-TRIMMING

Your Golden's nails should be trimmed once a month. This is one of the least favorite grooming chores, but do not neglect your dog's nails because nails

Start trimming your dog's nails while he is a puppy. With time, he'll get used to getting his nails cut as part of the normal grooming routine.

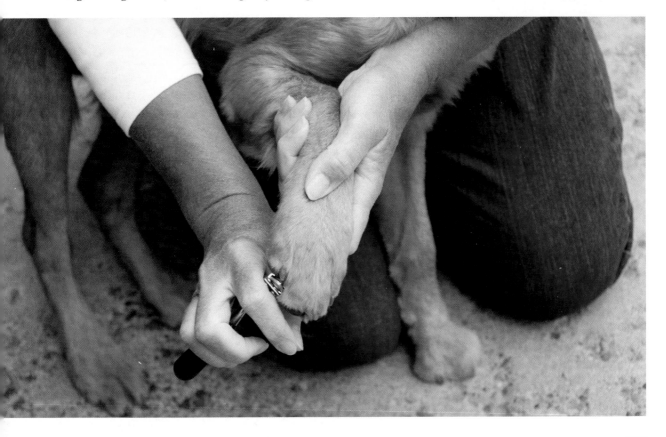

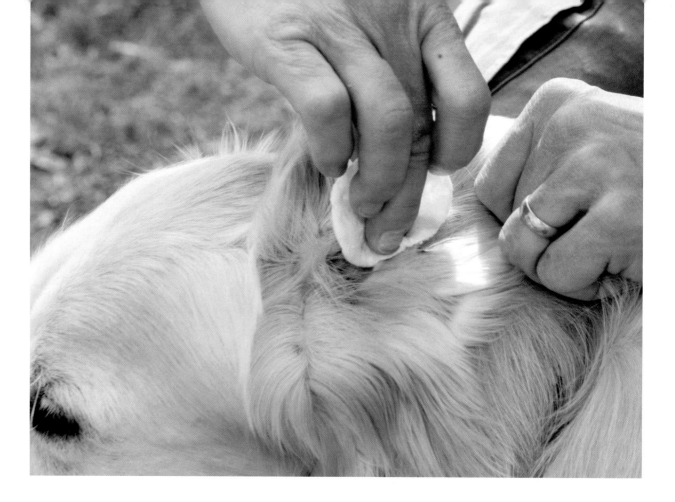

Use a cotton ball or small cotton pad to clean your Golden's ears. Don't probe too deeply, as the interior part of the ear is extremely sensitive.

that are too long can catch on things and scratch you. Early introduction to the trimming process is key. Puppies do not naturally like pedicures, so introduce nail-clipping as soon as possible. Try to make it a positive experience so that your dog at least tolerates it without a major battle. Offer treats each time so he will associate nail-clipping with food rewards.

At first, you may only be able to clip one or two nails at a time before your Golden tries to wrestle away from you. That's a good start. It is better to trim off a small amount of the nail more frequently than to cut back a nail that has grown too long. Clip off just the tip of the nail or trim at the curve of the nail. Be careful not to cut the quick (the pink vein in the nail) because it is painful, and the nail may bleed. If your Golden has light-colored nails, it will be easy to see the quick and avoid it, but if your dog has dark nails, it's best to just cut off a small amount each month so as not to accidentally cut too close. If you happen to snip the quick, you can stanch the bleeding with a few drops of clotting solution or with a styptic pen or powder. Keep it on hand; accidents happen.

EAR CARE

Check your dog's ears weekly. Are they clean and fresh smelling? Check for any foreign objects that may get stuck in his ear flap or ear canal. When walking or playing outside, seeds, burs, and foxtails can often get stuck in your Golden's fur and ears. If left in his ears, these objects will cause pain and could even damage your Golden's hearing. If you think something is stuck in your dog's ear, but you can't get it out, take your Golden to the vet right away. Your veterinarian will have the right tools to remove the object safely.

Dog Grooming Shopping List

Here are the items you need to groom your Golden Retriever:

BATHING

☐ A handheld spray attachment for your tub or sink

☐ A rubber mat for the dog to stand on

☐ A tearless dog shampoo and conditioner (don't use human products)

☐ Towels (a chamois is best)

☐ A pet hair dryer (you can use your own, but set it on low)

☐ Spritz-on dry shampoo (handy in case you need a quick cleanup to get rid of dirt or odor)

BRUSHING COAT

☐ Pin brush and slicker brush

☐ Stainless-steel comb

TRIMMING NAILS

☐ Dog nail cutters (scissor- or guillotine-type)

☐ Nail file or grinder

☐ Styptic powder or cornstarch (in case you cut the quick)

BRUSHING TEETH

☐ Dog toothbrush or rough washcloth

☐ Dog toothpaste (don't use human toothpaste)

CLEANING EARS

☐ Cotton balls or wipes

☐ Liquid ear-cleaning solution

WIPING EYES

☐ Dog eye wipes

☐ Cotton balls

Your veterinarian will check your Golden Retriever's ears every time he or she examines him. Ask your vet to show you the proper way to clean the ears. Ear infections are common in all dog breeds. Symptoms of ear infection include redness and/or swelling of the ear flap or inner ear, a nasty odor, or dark waxy discharge. The Golden Retriever's ear flaps keep the ear canal moist, especially in humid climates, which promotes musty growths. Regular cleaning with a specially formulated ear cleaner from your vet will keep your dog's ears clean and odor-free. Use a cotton ball or pad to clean the ear flap and the folds of the inner ear. Do not probe into the ear deeply or you might injure the ear drum.

The two most common mistakes owners make when dealing with an ear infection are waiting too long to seek treatment and failing to treat the ear for the entire course of medication, which then allows the infection to recur. Be proactive with your Golden's ear care—the better he'll hear you say, "Let's go for a walk!"

Remember that many dogs grow deaf with age. If your senior Golden no longer comes running at the clinking of the doggy treat jar, he may have a hearing problem. Time and experience will show you what changes and allowances to make if your dog develops hearing loss.

DENTAL HEALTH

When grooming your Golden Retriever, don't forget his glistening smile. Danger signs in your dog's mouth include yellow and brown tartar buildup along the gum line; red, inflamed gums; and persistent bad breath. Untreated, these conditions will allow bacteria to accumulate in your dog's mouth and enter his bloodstream through damaged gums, increasing the risk for disease in vital organs such as the heart, liver, and kidneys. Veterinarians tell us that periodontal disease can lead to kidney disease, a common cause of death in older dogs. Brushing your dog's teeth regularly can actually save his life.

Your vet should examine your Golden's teeth and gums during his annual checkup to make sure they are clean and healthy. He or she may recommend professional cleaning if there is excessive plaque buildup.

During the other 364 days of the year, you are your dog's dentist. Brush his teeth frequently, which means at least twice a week. Use a dog toothbrush and dog toothpaste, which is often flavored with chicken, beef, and liver. Once your dog gets used to you poking around in his mouth, he will enjoy (or at least tolerate) the gush of hamburger flavoring he tastes in his mouth. Don't use human toothpaste on your dog, as its contents can be harmful to dogs. If your dog resists a toothbrush, try a rough washcloth or gauze pad wrapped around your finger.

You can also help keep your dog's teeth clean by feeding him dry dog food. Hard foods like kibble help minimize plaque accumulation. Some dogs like raw vegetables like carrots which can help scrub away plaque while providing extra vitamins A and C. Invest in healthy chew objects, such as nylon or rubber bones and toys with ridges that act as tartar scrapers.

GET IN THE HABIT

Once you establish a habit of good grooming, Golden Retriever care is easy! All it takes is a bit of practice to get both you and your Golden accustomed to regular

brushing, nail-trimming, and ear cleaning. By brushing your Golden every other day, and every day during his shedding seasons, his coat will stay healthy and shiny throughout his life. Regular grooming is also a great way to check over your Golden Retriever's body for any changes that you may want to bring up to your vet. Grooming is a big part of your Golden's health care; spending a little time each day keeping your dog clean and well groomed contributes to your Golden Retriever's ongoing health.

Even with good ear care throughout their lives, older dogs often lose their hearing. Talk to your vet if you suspect your Golden is going deaf.

At a Glance ...

Golden Retrievers have two major shedding seasons, in the spring and fall; however, Goldens shed throughout the year. Brush your Golden Retriever every day during the shdding seasons and every other day the rest of the year.

. . . .

When you brush your Golden, do a thorough check of his body for any lumps, hot spots, or rashes. Check his eyes, ears, nose, and teeth for any redness, swelling, or other abnormalities. Grooming sessions are a great time to give your Golden a once-over; consult your veterinarian if you find anything that concerns you.

. . . .

Dental health is extremely important for your Golden's overall health. Regularly brushing your dog's teeth will help prevent tartar and plaque buildup and gum disease. Taking care of your dog's teeth may even add three to five years to your Golden's life.

CHAPTER TEN

Healthy Is Happy

All dog people know that you grow to love your dog more with each passing year. If you are lucky enough to have a Golden Retriever live to enjoy his "golden" years, you will know how deep your affection can become. How can you repay your Golden for all twelve, thirteen, fourteen or more years of happiness? Invest in your Golden's health from the very start!

Be proactive and informed. Don't wait for health problems to occur. The most effective way

to keep your dog healthy is to start your Golden on a preventive health-care program when he's a puppy and continue with it throughout his life.

WEIGHT WATCHERS

One area where owners can make a significant impact on their dog's health is weight control. According to *Veterinary Practice News* magazine, over half of the dogs vets see in their clinics are overweight—not really a shocking trend when you consider the prevalence of obesity among humans. However, unlike people, who regularly "super-size" meals, our dogs do not have a choice of what or how much they eat. Extra weight on your Golden Retriever can steal two or three years off his life. Here are words for you and your dog to live by: stay lean, live longer.

To determine whether or not your dog is overweight, stand over him and look down at him. Is there a waistline? (Yes, Goldens have waistlines just like Whippets and Poodles, though not as pronounced.) Now look at your dog from the side. You should see an apparent tuck-up under his belly. Now place your hands on his rib cage. There should be a thin layer of muscle over his ribs, and you should be able to feel his ribs when you press lightly. If your fingers sink through a layer of fat before you reach his ribs, it's time to start thinking about weight management strategies for your Golden.

First, talk with your veterinarian about the ways you can help your dog safely lose weight. Choose a low-calorie dog food and give him carrots as treats instead of dog cookies. Exercise more often. The key to safe weight loss is gradual weight loss. Don't try to shed those pounds all at once! It may take a few months to get your Golden Retriever back on the lean, healthy track, but your dog will be healthier and happier as a result.

CORE Vaccines
Check with your vet, but all puppies should receive vaccines for the following diseases:

CONDITION	TREATMENT	PROGNOSIS	VACCINE NEEDED
ADENOVIRUS-2 (immunizes against Adenovirus-1, the agent of infectious canine hepatitis)	No curative therapy for infectious hepatitis; treatment geared toward minimizing neurologic effects, shock, hemorrhage, secondary infections	Self-limiting but cross-protects against infectious hepatitis, which is highly contagious and can be mild to rapidly fatal	Recommended
DISTEMPER	No specific treatment; supportive treatment (IV fluids, antibiotics)	High mortality rates	Highly recommended
PARVOVIRUS-2	No specific treatment; supportive treatment (IV fluids, antibiotics)	Highly contagious to young puppies; high mortality rates	Highly recommended
RABIES	No treatment	Fatal	Required

A GOLDEN VETERINARIAN

A good veterinarian is worth his weight in gold—and Golden good health! He will be your puppy's doctor and friend, and your canine health-care educator. Find a good vet before you bring your puppy home. Because it's important that your vet live fairly close to your home—within at least 10 miles—you should be able to significantly narrow down your choices. Seek recommendations from responsible dog owners in your area or talk to people in a local all-breed or obedience club. A good vet will plan your puppy's long-term health care and help you become smarter about how to keep your Golden Retriever healthy.

Be sure to take your puppy to the veterinarian within a few days of picking him up from the breeder. Share any health records that the breeder provided, including vaccinations, worming protocol, and diet. You should also bring in a fecal sample for a worm test. The vet will thoroughly examine your Golden to assure you that he's in good health. He or she will listen to your dog's heart and lungs;

A PIECE OF HISTORY

Unlike the history of many breeds, the beginnings of the Golden Retriever are so well recorded, we even know the names of the very first dogs. A record book from 1840 to 1890 from Lord Tweedmouth's kennel was made public in 1952 and later published. Nous, the original yellow Wavy-Coated Retriever was bred to Belle, the Tweed Water Spaniel, to produce four yellow pups: Cowslip, Primrose, Crocus, and Ada. Why not name your Golden after one of the original four!

feel his abdomen, muscles, and joints; check his eyes and ears; and look inside his mouth and at the condition of his teeth and gums. Your vet will also ask you questions about your Golden Retriever's eating habits, bathroom habits, and overall personality and disposition. If you have any specific questions that you want to ask the veterinarian, write them down before your appointment—otherwise, you may forget to ask something important. No matter what, try to keep the appointment positive and comfortable for your new puppy. This is the first of many veterinary appointments that your dog will have in his lifetime, and the experience should be calm and welcoming.

Even if your Golden seems perfectly healthy, it's best to see the veterinarian at least once a year for a basic physical exam. As your dog gets older, around the age of seven or eight, it's best to take him to the vet for a checkup at least twice a year. Preventive care is the best type of health care. Your vet may spot something that you overlooked in your weekly grooming sessions, such as unhealthy gums

Canine Emergencies

For everyday commonsense care, every dog owner should know the signs of an emergency. Many dog agencies, humane societies, and animal shelters sponsor canine first aid seminars. Participants learn how to recognize and deal with signs of common emergency situations, how to assemble a first aid kit, how to give CPR to a dog, and more. The lesson here is: know your Golden Retriever. Early detection of any health problem is the key to your dog's longevity and quality of life.

Signs of an emergency include vomiting for more than twenty-four hours, bloody or prolonged (over twenty-four hours) diarrhea, fever (normal canine temperature is 101.5 degrees Fahrenheit), and a sudden swelling of the head or any body part (allergic reaction to an insect bite or other stimulus).

Some symptoms of other more common emergency situations include:

Heatstroke: Excessive panting, drooling, rapid pulse, dark reddened gums, and a frantic, glazed expression (you'll know it when you see it)

Hypothermia: Shivering, very pale gums and body temperature under 100 degrees Fahrenheit

Shock (due to severe blood loss from an injury): Shivering, weak pulse, weakness and listlessness, depression, and lowered body temperature

When in doubt, always get your dog to a veterinarian as soon as possible. Have the emergency clinic pre-programmed on your cell phone and be sure you know how to get there quickly and safely.

or dirty ears, a possible sign of ear mites. This is also a great time to talk with your vet about your dog's lifestyle and diet, asking his or her advice about the best ways to care for your Golden Retriever as he ages.

VACCINATIONS

At your first appointment, your veterinarian will talk to you about a schedule of vaccinations that your puppy still requires. Your breeder should have already started your puppy's vaccinations before you brought him home. All of your puppy's shots will be documented on the health records that your breeder provided you when you purchased your puppy. Bring these to the veterinarian at your Golden's first appointment so that your vet can decide how to continue your puppy's vaccination schedule. Although vaccination protocols differ among veterinarians, most recommend a series of "combination" shots given every three to four weeks. Combination shots are injections that include multiple vaccines in

Other Vaccines and Treatment

Depending on where you live and your dog's needs, the following ailments and diseases can be treated through your veterinarian:

CONDITION	TREATMENT	PROGNOSIS	RECOMMENDATION
BORDETELLA (KENNEL COUGH)	Keep warm; humidify room; moderate exercise	Highly contagious; rarely fatal in healthy dogs; easily treated	Optional vaccine; prevalence varies; vaccine may be linked to acute reactions; low efficacy
FLEA AND TICK INFESTATION	Topical and ingestible	Highly contagious	Preventive treatment highly recommended
HEARTWORM	Arsenical compound; rest; restricted exercise	Widely occurring infections; preventive programs available regionally; successful treatment after early detection	Preventive treatment highly recommended
INTESTINAL WORMS	Dewormer; home medication regimen	Good with prompt treatment	Preventive treatment highly recommended
LYME DISEASE (BORRELIOSIS)	Antibiotics	Can't completely eliminate the organism, but can be controlled in most cases	Vaccine recommended only for dogs with high risk of exposure to deer ticks
PARAINFLUENZA	Rest; humidify room; moderate exercise	Highly contagious; mild; self-limiting; rarely fatal	Optional but recommended; doesn't block infection, but lessens clinical signs
PERIODONTITIS	Dental cleaning; extractions; repair	Excellent, but involves anesthesia	Preventive treatment recommended

Don't Forget His Teeth!

Your dog's teeth are also an important part of his health care. In addition to regular brushing, have your vet examine your Golden Retriever's teeth during his annual checkup. Your veterinarian will let you know if your pup needs his pearly whites cleaned. If neglected, your dog's teeth will develop a buildup of tartar along the gum line that will cause gingivitis and tooth decay.

Periodontal disease is a major contributor to kidney disease; there is even a risk of damage to the heart, liver, and kidneys through bacteria that can enter your dog's bloodstream through his mouth. So keep on brushing—and don't forget to visit the veterinarian regularly!

each shot. Some breeders feel that combination shots are too strong for a young puppy's immature immune system, so they may recommend a series of vaccines given through individual injections. Talk with your vet about the pros and cons of combination shots and the possible risks to your puppy.

The American Veterinary Medical Association (AVMA) recommends a series of "core" vaccines. Core vaccines protect against serious diseases that are dangerous to all dogs throughout the country. The major core vaccines protect against diseases such as distemper, canine adenovirus, parvovirus, and rabies. All of these diseases are extremely contagious and have high mortality rates if contracted. The rabies vaccine is required by law in all fifty states and is usually given three to four weeks after the rest of your puppy's vaccinations.

Additional vaccines your veterinarian may suggest depend on where you live and your Golden's lifestyle. These optional but often recommended vaccines are called "non-core" vaccines. Non-core vaccines protect your Golden Retriever against regional diseases such as canine parainfluenza, leptospirosis, coronavirus, Bordetella (canine cough), and Lyme disease (borreliosis). Your veterinarian will let you know which of these non-core vaccines are recommended for your area, and which diseases your Golden is most at risk for.

Visit the American Animal Hospital Association's website at www.aahanet .org/Library/CanineVaccine.aspx for a detailed report on common core and non-core vaccines recommended for your puppy. The AVMA also has a helpful webpage about pet vaccinations at www.avma.org/issues/vaccination.

PESKY PESTS

Creepy critters have survived since the Mesozoic era, and today, fleas are unfortunately as inevitable in the life of modern man and dog as they were to our cavemen and wolf ancestors. Thanks to some fascinating flea fossils, scientists are fairly certain that even dinosaurs had fleas! However, your Golden won't care about all of this history when he contracts fleas that will likely force him to constantly itch, bite, and scratch himself for relief.

Fleas: For an outdoor dog like the Golden Retriever, it's a near impossible task to completely protect him from fleas. Fortunately, eradicating a flea infestation on your dog and in your home is relatively simple nowadays as compared to the stinky flea collars and powders of the past.

Ridding your Golden and home of fleas is a two-step process. You must first kill the adult fleas and eggs in your dog's environment (your home and backyard), and then you must kill the fleas and eggs on your dog. Your Golden's environment means outdoors as well as indoors, including furniture, carpeting, the dog's bedding, and so forth. An insect-growth-regulator spray and insecticide are required to kill adult fleas and any larvae they've deposited in their surroundings. To treat your dog, you can choose a pill or a liquid medication, the latter of which is squeezed onto the back of the dog's neck. The liquid spreads through your dog's bloodstream, effectively killing any flea that bites your dog. Discuss flea remedies with your breeder and your veterinarian. Some dogs have reactions to certain flea medications, so always monitor your dog after administering any pill or solution.

Ticks and Mites: More than just an uncomfortable nuisance for your Golden Retriever, ticks can carry disease. The deer tick causes Lyme disease (borreliosis); Dermacentor ticks spread Rocky Mountain spotted fever as well as Colorado tick fever; and the brown dog tick causes ehrlichiosis. If you live in an area where ticks are common, your veterinarian may suggest a few extra vaccinations to protect your Golden from these diseases. There are tens of thousands of mite species, which often attack your dogs' ears. They also can aggravate atopic dermatitis, a kind of eczema believed to be caused by fleas that affects both humans and dogs. Mites are easily treatable with a prescription medication from your veterinarian.

Worms: Now on to internal parasites! Roundworms, tapeworms, hookworms, and whipworms are the most common parasites found in dogs. Most puppies are born with roundworm larvae, passed on in utero or through the mother's milk. Breeders usually worm puppies twice prior to sending them to new homes. A stool sample will provide evidence of most worms, as tapeworms and roundworms can be seen with the naked eye—tapeworm segments look like moving grains of rice, and roundworms look like strands of cooked spaghetti. Dogs with a worm infestation may vomit, have diarrhea, lose weight, have dry hair, and look generally ragged. If you suspect that your dog may have worms, take him to the vet for treatment as soon as possible. Your vet may suggest an over-the-counter dewormer or prescribe a stronger medication to help your Golden Retriever stay parasite-free.

Heartworms: Heartworms are the most serious parasites found in dogs; they gather in your dog's heart and are often fatal if left untreated. Contracted through mosquito bites, all dogs are at risk for heartworms no matter where they

live. Your vet will most likely suggest that your dog take a heartworm preventive of some sort. These preventives are available by prescription in pill and shot form; your vet will decide which is best for your dog and his lifestyle.

BOTH EYES ON THE GOLDEN

No breeder, veterinarian, or psychic can guarantee any dog's ongoing health. But the one person who has the most impact on your dog's well-being is you! You see your dog every day, letting him run in the yard, taking him for a walk, feeding and watering him, brushing his coat and his teeth, and spending quiet time with him. All of these everyday activities present opportunities for you to observe your dog

Support Canine Health Research

The mission of the American Kennel Club Canine Health Foundation, Inc. (AKC CHF) is to advance the health of all dogs by funding sound scientific research and supporting the dissemination of health information to prevent, treat, and cure canine disease. The foundation makes grants to fund:

- Identifying the cause(s) of disease
- Earlier, more accurate diagnosis
- Developing screening tests for breeders
- Accurate, positive prognosis
- Effective, efficient treatment

The AKC CHF also supports educational programs that bring scientists together to discuss their work and develop new collaborations to further advance canine health.

The AKC created the foundation in 1995 to raise funds to support canine health research. Each year, the AKC CHF allocates $1.5 million to new health-research projects.

How You Can Help: If you have an AKC-registered dog, submit his DNA sample (cheek swab or blood sample) to the Canine Health Information Center (CHIC) DNA databank (www.caninehealthinfo.org). Encourage regular health testing by breeders, get involved with your local dog club, and support the efforts to host health education programs. And, if possible, make a donation.

For information, contact the AKC Canine Health Foundation, P.O. Box 900061, Raleigh, NC 27675-9061 or check out the website at www.akcchf.org.

and his health. Look for changes in his appearance, behavior, appetite, gait, and moods. If you notice anything out of the ordinary, call your vet for advice.

Playtime: Is your Golden Retriever moving slower than usual? Is he limping or favoring one side or the other? Is he lethargic or short of breath during a walk? Is he carrying his tail down?

Mealtime: Is he less interested in eating? Is your Golden drinking more water than usual? Has he been gaining or losing weight? Is he drooling?

Potty Time: Is he going to the bathroom more than usual or straining when he tries to relieve himself?

Grooming Time: Is your dog cocking his head to the left or right? Is he sensitive when you touch his ears, mouth, legs, or feet? Are his teeth clean and his breath good smelling? Are there any lumps or abnormalities under his coat? Are his eyes watery?

All the Time: Is he unusually lethargic or disinterested in affection? Is he licking his feet or biting at himself? Is your Golden Retriever restless or pacing around? Is he barking more than usual? Whining or whimpering?

IT'S UP TO YOU

Your Golden Retriever relies entirely on you to keep him both mentally and physically healthy and happy. Grooming, feeding, and exercise are just the beginning. Your veterinarian is the best resource for advice on feeding, care, and exercise for your Golden. With your veterinarian's help and regular health-care visits, your Golden Retriever will share many years of health and happiness with you and your family.

Health care is especially important during your dog's senior years. Keep a close eye on your Golden for any peculiar behaviors or symptoms and don't hesitate to ask your veterinarian if you have any questions.

At a Glance ...

Keep a close eye on your Golden Retriever's weight. A healthy, nutritious diet and daily exercise will help keep your dog fit and lean. If you notice that your dog is putting on pounds, talk with your veterinarian about alternative diets and exercise for healthy weight loss.

. . . .

Before bringing your puppy home, choose a veterinarian whom you trust. A good veterinarian will be an asset to you for advice throughout your Golden Retriever's life.

. . . .

At your first office visit, your veterinarian will talk to you about a vaccination schedule for your puppy. Ask about vaccines that are required and recommended for your area.

. . . .

Grooming, diet, and exercise are only the beginning of preventive care for your Golden Retriever. Annual health-care visits with your Golden's veterinarian will help spot any health issues as early as possible.

CHAPTER ELEVEN

Go for the Gold

So many activities await you and your Golden Retriever! Whether it's a long walk—or swim—at the beach or a run around the course at a local agility trial or a therapy dog visit to a hospital, you will find rewards and a ton of fun in the time spent with your well-trained Golden. Your dog's handsome looks, sweet temperament, and advanced education will be appreciated by judges, dog fanciers, nursing-home residents, sports fans, beach bums, and

everyone else you and your dog meet on the way to an active, happy life together.

OUT AND ABOUT

Golden Retrievers love running around the backyard eyeing sparrows and chasing squirrels, but getting out there and seeing the world is much more exciting. Taking your Golden puppy on a long walk is the best exercise for him. Once he's a year old and if he's in good physical condition, you can jog or cycle together as well. It's best to jog on turf or other soft surface that is easy on your Golden's joints and feet.

Keep in mind that until your dog is a year old, you should avoid any activity that will stress his growing bones. A young Golden Retriever's bones are soft and still form-ing, and thus more vulnerable to injury during his first year of life. Youngsters should not be subjected to heavy stress. That means shorter walks and no jumping or wrestling games that can hurt or twist his structure.

Given the Golden Retriever's love of water, swimming is the perfect activ-ity at any age. Unlike your kids, Goldens don't need a couple of summers at the YMCA to learn how to become reliable swimmers. Most Goldens live to fetch a ball, Frisbee, or other toy in the water. Be sure that you're aware of changing tides or rip currents when allowing your dog to dive into the ocean. Rinse him off once he gets home to remove the salt and any ocean contaminants from his coat. Safety always has to come before (and after) fun!

BEST IN SHOW

Dog shows have been around since the nineteenth century and have never been more popular than they are today. The American Kennel Club sponsors nearly 4,000 all-breed and specialty shows annually. These shows range in size from small local shows with a couple hundred entries to large all-breed shows that attract thousands of entries. The AKC/Eukanuba National Championship Show in 2011 boasted nearly 4,000 entries.

Golden Retrievers are popular show dogs, but surprisingly, they are rarely contenders for Best in Show. No Golden has ever won the top prize at the pres-tigious Westminster Kennel Club Dog Show or the Crufts Dog Show in Britain. Despite these statistics, Goldens are crowd-pleasers at dog shows and easy to exhibit. They are quite glamorous with their luxurious coats, feathering on the body and tail, and their sweet expressions. Of course, a well-bred Golden can sail around the ring, showing off his effortless gait, and always gets rousing applause during the Group judging.

Dog shows are called conformation shows because the judge is evaluating the dogs by how well they *conform* to the breed standard. The Golden Retriever that most closely resembles the dog described in the breed standard is selected as the winner and awarded Best of Breed. All Best of Breed winners then compete in their respective Groups. In other words, all of the Sporting breeds—including the

Golden Retrievers are water dogs through and through. If your dog loves the water, consider taking him to the lake or the beach for some exercise.

Golden—compete against each other. Once all seven groups have been judged, those Group winners compete for Best in Show, the most prestigious award.

Tell your breeder that you are interested in getting involved in conformation, so your breeder can help you choose a puppy with show potential. The breeder will explain all the necessary steps—including care, training, and costs—to get you started in the sport. Because the purpose of conformation is to promote and breed new generations of dogs that conform to their breed standard, all dogs that compete in dog shows must not be spayed or neutered. For more information on how to get involved in dog shows with your Golden Retriever, visit the AKC website, www.akc.org/events/conformation.

OBEDIENCE AND AGILITY TRIALS

AKC obedience trials began in 1936; while AKC agility trials have only been around since 1994. But in that short period of time, agility has surpassed obedience in popularity. There are about seven times as many AKC agility trials as there are obedience trials. Nevertheless, both are exciting to participate in and to watch, and any dog can compete, whether purebred or mixed, altered or not. Be sure to visit a dog show where obedience and agility trials are being held so you can see the dogs and their handlers in action. Don't be surprised if a few very talented Goldens are leading the pack!

The best way to get involved in either sport is to join a training group in your area. Training groups have all of the obstacles and equipment necessary for training, and experienced handlers and trainers are always happy to assist new owners. The energy of obedience and agility competitors is truly infectious, and

Did You Know?

Golden Retrievers were first shown in the 1908 Crystal Palace Dog Show. The Crystal Palace Dog Show in London was the largest dog show held before the Westminster Kennel Club Dog Show in New York surpassed it in 1905.

Golden Retrievers excel in the high-energy sport of agility. Sailing over obstacles with ease, your Golden may enjoy the excitement and challenge of this popular sport.

their enthusiasm for the sport will give you the extra incentive to keep training and competing with your Golden.

In both sports, the dog must respond to the owner's cues as he moves through the course. Obedience trials include exercises like scent discrimination, short retrieves, the long stay, hurdles, broad jump, and sitting in a group. Agility trials are more like obstacle courses, requiring the dogs to literally jump through hoops as well as walk over teeter-totters, across balance beams, through tunnels, and more. There are different levels of difficulty in both obedience and agility, and each level comes with new obstacles and more challenging tasks.

Junior Scholarships

The American Kennel Club shows its commitment to supporting young people in their interest in purebred dogs by awarding thousands of dollars in scholarships to those competing in Junior Showmanship. The scholarships range from $1,000 to $5,000 and are based on a person's academic achievements and his or her history with purebred dogs. Learn more at www.akc.org/kids_juniors.

In obedience, points are awarded based on the difficulty level of each task, and in the more advanced levels, owners may only use hand signals to cue their dogs. Agility is based purely on speed and the successful navigation of the course obstacles. For more information on how to get involved in obedience or agility with your Golden Retriever, visit the AKC website at www.akc.org/events/obedience or www.akc.org/events/agility.

AKC RALLY®

A stepping stone between the Canine Good Citizen test and the world of agility is AKC's newest sport Rally, which is based on the rally style of car racing. Rally involves the precision of obedience and the fast-paced excitement of agility. Handlers and their dogs must work their way through a course comprised of ten or twenty signs, each of which gives a direction like "Stop and Down," "Slow Forward from Sit," or "Double Left About-Turn." The handler talks to his dog as much as possible, calling cues and cheering him on, and the dog does not have to heel perfectly as he follows his handler around the course. The only rule is that the handler may not touch the dog. Rally is not as competitive as obedience or agility and is geared more toward pet owners than the more dedicated competitor. Its main goal is to promote teamwork between owner and dog and to produce well-behaved dogs that are mannerly at home, in public places, and with other dogs. Dogs must be six months of age to participate. To learn more about Rally, visit www.akc.org/events/rally.

HUNTING TESTS AND FIELD TRIALS

What better way to exercise your Golden than doing what the breed was born to do—retrieve! A Golden's love of bird work can range from moderate to wildly passionate, but almost every Golden Retriever will enjoy time spent working in the field. AKC sponsors hunting tests, which are designed for the noncompetitive sportsman who may or may not actually hunt. Your local breed or retriever club can refer you to groups that train specifically for these events.

By far the most challenging and difficult of all sporting-dog events, field trials are specifically designed to challenge retrievers' natural talents in the field. Even though Labradors dominate the field-trial scene, Goldens excel in this very competitive sport as well. If you hope to be successful in field trials, make sure you have chosen a pup that comes from hunting stock. Field trials are much more intense than hunting tests. In field trials, retrievers are judged on how well they mark (or remember) the location of a downed bird and return it to their handlers and how well they retrieve a sight-unseen planted bird directed only by hand, voice, and whistle signals.

Both hunting tests and field trials can vary in difficulty, from marking a single bird to marking multiple birds and finding blind retrieves (unmarked birds) from short to long distances. Newcomers are encouraged to find a retriever club that offers support and instruction by hunting enthusiasts. To learn more about hunting tests and field trials, visit the GRCA website at www.grca.org or the AKC website at www.akc.org/events/hunting_tests/retrievers or www.akc.org/events/field_trials/retrievers.

OTCH! That's Smart!

Any obedience-trial competitor will tell you that achieving an OTCH with his or her Golden involves a lot of hard work. OTCH is the prefix for Obedience Trial Champion, a title instituted by the AKC in 1977. In dog obedience circles, the OTCH is known as the "PhD for Dogs!" The first Golden Retriever to add OTCH to his name was Moreland's Golden Tonka, handled by his owner Russ Klipple of Pennsylvania.

The National Obedience Championship title (NOC) is awarded to only one dog each year, the winner of the AKC National Obedience Championship held each December. In 2011, the National Obedience Champion was Spirit's Zim Zam Zoom, a Golden Retriever from North Vancouver owned by Ward Falkner. The three runners-up were all Goldens as well.

The AKC Code of Sportsmanship

- Sportsmen respect the history, traditions, and integrity of the sport of purebred dogs.
- Sportsmen commit themselves to values of fair play, honesty, courtesy, and vigorous competition, as well as winning and losing with grace.
- Sportsmen refuse to compromise their commitment and obligation to the sport of purebred dogs by injecting personal advantage or consideration into their decisions or behavior.
- The sportsman judge judges only on the merits of the dogs and considers no other factors.
- The sportsman judge or exhibitor accepts constructive criticism.
- The sportsman exhibitor declines to enter or exhibit under a judge where it might reasonably appear that the judge's placements could be based on something other than the merits of the dogs.
- The sportsman exhibitor refuses to compromise the impartiality of a judge.
- The sportsman respects the American Kennel Club's bylaws, rules, regulations, and policies governing the sport of purebred dogs.
- Sportsmen find that vigorous competition and civility are not inconsistent and are able to appreciate the merit of their competition and the efforts of competitors.
- Sportsmen welcome, encourage, and support newcomers to the sport.
- Sportsmen will deal fairly with all those who trade with them.
- Sportsmen are willing to share honest and open appraisals of both the strengths and weaknesses of their breeding stock.
- Sportsmen spurn any opportunity to take personal advantage of positions offered or bestowed upon them.
- Sportsmen always consider as paramount the welfare of their dogs.
- Sportsmen refuse to embarrass the sport, the American Kennel Club, or themselves while taking part in the sport.

SEARCH AND RESCUE

There are many types of search and rescue dogs, including airscenting, water search, avalanche, disaster, and cadaver search. Golden Retrievers, as well as other breeds of Sporting and Working dogs, often make responsible and capable search and rescue dogs due to their trainability and love of humans. Disasters such as the September 11th attacks on the World Trade Center or Hurricane Katrina have brought publicity to the abilities and talents of canine search and rescue teams. Training your dog to be a search and rescue dog is a full-time job. Rescue dogs and their handlers must be available seven days a week, fifty-two weeks a year, and be able to supply their own equipment and provide their own means of travel. If you are interested in learning more, visit the National Disaster Search Dog Foundation (NDSDF) website, www.searchdogfoundation.org, or the National Search Dog Alliance (NSDA) website, www.n-sda.org.

MACH and PACH

Agility dogs have more titles to compete for than any other dogs. At the top of the long list are MACH and PACH. The Master Agility Champion (MACH) prefix is awarded to a dog that has earned a minimum of 750 championship points and 20 double qualifying scores in Excellent B Standard agility class and the Excellent B Jumpers with Weaves class.

The new prefix PACH (Preferred Agility Champion) was created to recognize the superior performance, speed, and consistency of AKC's Preferred Agility competitors and requires that dogs earn the same as MACH dogs in the Preferred class.

THERAPY

How can you share the joys of your special Golden Retriever with other people? Consider therapy work. Dogs that love people make the best therapy dogs, and a Golden Retriever definitely fits that description! Thanks to their outgoing personalities, evidenced by their ever-wagging tails and always-present smiles, Goldens make natural therapy dogs.

If you're interested in visiting nursing homes, hospitals, and other care centers to share your Golden with people in need, then get your dog registered as a therapy dog. Obedience-trained, mannerly Golden Retrievers make ideal canine ambassadors. The AKC Canine Good Citizen test is a good place to start, as most

Service Dogs

Golden Retrievers are often seen serving as assistance dogs in the community. All retriever breeds, but especially Goldens and Labrador Retrievers, are most often selected as service dogs. A "service dog" or "assistance dog" is the generic name for dogs trained to help a physically challenged person. A service dog must be able to endure inclement weather, distance walking, and have the ability to perform simple tasks. A Golden Retriever can do all of these things and more. So when you see a Golden wearing a service vest, you'll know right away that his human is in good paws.

Seeing Eye Dog: A Seeing Eye dog is trained from puppyhood as a guide for people who are blind or visually impaired. These dogs wear special harnesses that allow their owners to feel their dogs stop or move around certain obstacles for safety and mobility. Seeing Eye dogs are trained by generous foster owners who eventually place their dogs in needed homes.

Psychiatric Service Dog: These dogs can be life-changing for people with mental disabilities. For example, someone with agoraphobia, the fear of open spaces, may be able to venture out in public with a Golden Retriever specially trained never to leave the handler's side. An autistic person can benefit from a service dog trained to alert him or her to repetitive movements associated with autism, such as hand flopping.

Seizure Alert/Response Dog: This dog is trained to respond to certain cues that a seizure is about to strike his human, and to either stay with the person or go get help. Some dogs are trained to touch a speed-dial button on the phone that dials 911 and to start barking when he hears a voice at the other end of the receiver.

Golden Retrievers make wonderful service dogs because of their intelligence, sensitivity, and people-loving personalities. Most are trained by dedicated volunteers.

registries require dogs to know all ten of the behaviors on the test, and some even require the Canine Good Citizen title.

The AKC Therapy Dog program awards an official title, AKC ThD, to any registered therapy dog that performs a certain number of visits per year. The American Kennel Club works with over fifty-five organizations that register therapy dogs, including the Pet Partners Program (www.petpartners.org), Therapy Dogs Inc. (www.therapydogs.com), and Therapy Dogs International (www.tdi-dog.org). Each registry has different criteria for registration. For more information, visit www.akc.org/akctherapydog.

A GOLDEN BOND

Your Golden Retriever's favorite activity is anything that he gets to do with you, his favorite person. No matter which activities you choose to pursue with your dog, whether it is agility, obedience, therapy, hunt tests, or simply daily jogging or hiking, your Golden will be overjoyed to spend time with you. Plus, getting involved in the community with your dog is a great way to meet other dog-owners like you. Even if your Golden Retriever never wins a conformation ribbon or agility trophy, he will always be a gold medalist in your heart, and a treasured member of your family.

At a Glance ...

Due to their retriever instincts and devotion to their owners, Golden Retrievers excel in the AKC sports of obedience, agility, and Rally. Check out the websites of the American Kennel Club (www .akc.org) and the Golden Retriever Club of America (www.grca.org) for more information on how to get involved in organized dog sports.

If your well-behaved Golden passed the Canine Good Citizen test with ease, you can share the joy that your Golden brings you with those in need. Consider becoming a therapy dog team, a great way to get your Golden involved in the community.

Your Golden Retriever needs daily exercise to keep him mentally and physically healthy. Whether it be a daily jog, bike ride, or rousing game of fetch, your Golden only wants to spend time with you—and he will be happier and healthier for it!

Resources

BOOKS

The American Kennel Club's Meet the Breeds: Dog Breeds from A to Z, 2012 edition (Irvine, California: BowTie Press, 2011) The ideal puppy buyer's guide, this book has all you need to know about each breed currently recognized by the AKC.

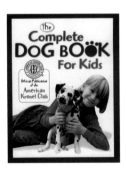

The Complete Dog Book, 20th edition (New York: Ballantine Books, 2006) This official publication of the AKC, first published in 1929, includes the complete histories and breed standards of 153 recognized breeds, as well as information on general care and the dog sport.

The Complete Dog Book for Kids (New York: Howell Book House, 1996) Specifically geared toward young people, this official publication of the AKC presents 149 breeds and varieties, as well as introductory owners' information.

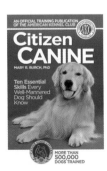

Citizen Canine: Ten Essential Skills Every Well-Mannered Dog Should Know by Mary R. Burch, PhD (Freehold, New Jersey: Kennel Club Books, 2010) This official AKC publication is the definitive guide to the AKC's Canine Good Citizen® Program, recognized as the gold standard of behavior for dogs, with more than half a million dogs trained.

DOGS: The First 125 Years of the American Kennel Club (Freehold, New Jersey: Kennel Club Books, 2009) This official AKC publication presents an authoritative, complete history of the AKC, including detailed information not found in any other volume.

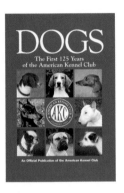

Dog Heroes of September 11th: A Tribute to America's Search and Rescue Dogs, 10th anniversary edition, by Nona Kilgore Bauer (Freehold, New Jersey: Kennel Club Books, 2011) A publication to salute the canines that served in the recovery missions following the September 11th attacks, this book serves as a lasting tribute to these noble American heroes.

The Original Dog Bible: The Definitive Source for All Things Dog, 2nd edition, by Kristin Mehus-Roe (Irvine, California: BowTie Press, 2009) This 831-page magnum opus includes more than 250 breed profiles, hundreds of color photographs, and a wealth of information on every dog topic imaginable—thousands of practical tips on grooming, training, care, and much more.

PERIODICALS

American Kennel Club Gazette

Every month since 1889, serious dog fanciers have looked to the *AKC Gazette* for authoritative advice on training, showing, breeding, and canine health. Each issue includes the breed columns section, written by experts from the respective breed clubs. Only available electronically.

AKC Family Dog

This is a bimonthly magazine for the dog lover whose special dog is "just a pet." Helpful tips, how-tos, and features are written in an entertaining and reader-friendly format. It's a lifestyle magazine for today's busy families who want to enjoy a rewarding, mutually happy relationship with their canine companions.

Dog Fancy

The world's most widely read dog magazine, *Dog Fancy* celebrates dogs and the people who love them. Each monthly issue includes info on cutting-edge medical developments, health and fitness (with a focus on prevention, treatment, and natural therapy), behavior and training, travel and activities, breed profiles and dog news, issues and trends for purebred and mixed-breed dog owners. The magazine informs, inspires, and entertains while promoting responsible dog ownership. Throughout its more than forty-year history, *Dog Fancy* has garnered numerous honors, including being named the Best All-Breed Magazine by the Dog Writers Association of America.

Dogs in Review

For more than fifteen years, *Dogs in Review* has showcased the finest dogs in the United States and from around the world. The emphasis has always been on strong content, with input from distinguished breeders, judges, and handlers worldwide. This global perspective distinguishes this monthly publication from its competitors—no other North American dog-show magazine gathers together so many international experts to enlighten and entertain its readership.

Dogs USA

Dogs USA is an annual lifestyle magazine published by the editors of *Dog Fancy* that covers all aspects of the dog world: culture, art, history, travel, sports, and science. It also profiles breeds to help prospective owners choose the best dogs for their future needs, such as a potential show champion, super service dog, great pet, or competitive star.

Natural Dog

Natural Dog is the magazine dedicated to giving a dog a natural lifestyle. From nutritional choices to grooming to dog-supply options, this publication helps readers make the transition from traditional to natural methods. The magazine also explores the array of complementary treatments available for today's dogs: acupuncture,

massage, homeopathy, aromatherapy, and much more. *Natural Dog* appears as an annual publication and also as the flip side of *Dog Fancy* magazine four times a year (in February, May, August, and November).

Puppies USA

From the editors of *Dog Fancy* as well, this annual magazine offers essential information for all new puppy owners. *Puppies USA* is lively and informative, including advice on general care, nutrition, grooming, and training techniques for all puppies, whether purebred or mixed breed, adopted, rescued, or purchased. It also offers family fun through quizzes, contests, and more. An extensive breeder directory is included.

WEBSITES

www.akc.org

The American Kennel Club's (AKC's) website is an excellent starting point for researching dog breeds and learning about puppy care. The site lists hundreds of breeders, along with basic information about breed selection and basic care. The site also has links to the national breed club of every AKC-recognized breed; breed-club sites offer plenty of detailed breed information, as well as lists of member breeders. In addition, you can find the AKC National Breed Club Rescue List at www.akc.org/breeds/rescue.cfm. If looking for purebred puppies, go to www.puppybuyerinfo.com for AKC classifieds and parent-club referrals.

www.dogchannel.com

Powered by *Dog Fancy*, Dog Channel is "the website for dog lovers," where hundreds of thousands of visitors each month find extensive information on breeds, training, health and nutrition, puppies, care, activities, and more. Interactive features include forums, Dog College, games, and Club Dog, a free club where dog lovers can create blogs for their pets and earn points to buy products. DogChannel is the one-stop site for all things dog.

www.meetthebreeds.com

The official website of the AKC Meet the Breeds® event, hosted by the American Kennel Club in the Jacob Javits Center in New York City in the fall. The first Meet the Breeds event took place in 2009. The website includes information on every recognized breed of dog and cat, alphabetically listed, as well as the breeders, demonstration facilitators, sponsors, and vendors participating in the annual event.

AKC AFFILIATES

The **AKC Museum of the Dog**, established in 1981, is located in St. Louis, Missouri, and houses the world's finest collection of art devoted to the dog. Visit www.museumofthedog.org.

The **AKC Humane Fund** promotes the joy and value of responsible and productive pet ownership through education, outreach, and grant-making. Monies raised may fund grants to organizations that teach responsible pet ownership; provide for the health and well-being of all dogs; and preserve and celebrate the human-animal bond and the evolutionary relationship between dogs and humankind. Go to www.akchumanefund.org.

The **American Kennel Club Companion Animal Recovery (CAR) Corporation** is dedicated to reuniting lost microchipped and tattooed pets with their owners. AKC CAR maintains a permanent-identification database and provides lifetime recovery services 24 hours a day, 365 days a year, for all animal species. Millions of pets are enrolled in the program, which was established in 1995. Visit www.akccar.org.

The **American Kennel Club Canine Health Foundation (AKC CHF), Inc.** is the largest foundation in the world to fund canine-only health studies for purebred and mixed-breed dogs. More than $22 million has been allocated in research funds to more than 500 health studies conducted to help dogs live longer, healthier lives. Go to www.akcchf.org.

AKC PROGRAMS

The **Canine Good Citizen Program (CGC)** was established in 1989 and is designed to recognize dogs that have good manners at home and in the community. This rapidly growing, nationally recognized program stresses responsible dog ownership for owners and basic training and good manners for dogs. All dogs that pass the ten-step Canine Good Citizen test receive a certificate from the American Kennel Club. Go to www.akc.org/events/cgc.

The **AKC S.T.A.R. Puppy Program** is designed to get dog owners and their puppies off to a good start and is aimed at loving dog owners who have taken the time to attend basic obedience classes with their puppies. After completing a six-week training course, the puppy must pass the AKC S.T.A.R. Puppy test, which evaluates Socialization, Training, Activity, and Responsibility. Go to www.akc.org/starpuppy.

The **AKC Therapy Dog** program recognizes all American Kennel Club dogs and their owners who have given their time and helped people by volunteering as a therapy dog-and-owner team. The AKC Therapy Dog program is an official American Kennel Club title awarded to dogs that have worked to improve the lives of the people they have visited. The AKC Therapy Dog title (AKC ThD) can be earned by dogs that have been certified by recognized therapy dog organizations. For more information, visit www.akc.org/akctherapydog.

Index

AMERICAN KENNEL CLUB®

Advocating for the purebred dog as a family companion, advancing canine health and well-being, working to protect the rights of all dog owners and promoting responsible dog ownership, the **American Kennel Club:**

Sponsors more than **22,000 sanctioned events** annually including conformation, agility, obedience, rally, tracking, lure coursing, earthdog, herding, field trial, hunt test, and coonhound events

Features a **10-step Canine Good Citizen® program** that rewards dogs who have good manners at home and in the community

Has reunited more than **400,000** lost pets with their owners through the AKC Companion Animal Recovery - visit **www.akccar.org**

Created and supports the AKC Canine Health Foundation, which funds research projects using the more than **$22 million** the AKC has donated since 1995 - visit **www.akcchf.org**

Joins **animal lovers** through education, outreach and grant-making via the AKC Humane Fund - visit **www.akchumanefund.org**

We're more than champion dogs. We're the dog's champion.

www.akc.org